TERRORISM AND THE AMERICAN RESPONSE

Alvin H. Buckelew

with foreword by
John P. East
United States Senate

MIRA Academic Press
San Rafael, California

Published in the United States of America by
    MIRA Academic Press
    P.O. Box 4334
    Civic Center Branch
    San Rafael, California 94914-4334

Printed and bound in the United States of
America.

ISBN 0-917919-00-9

Library of Congress Catalog Card Number: 84-61050

ACKNOWLEDGMENTS

I am indebted to a number of people who gave unselfishly of their time, encouragement, and assistance: Dr. Constantinos Beros; Dr. Sam Francis; Dr. Randy Hamilton; Egil Krogh; Bob Lamborn; Montgomery Littlefield; and Larry Sulc.

The people to whom I owe special appreciation for their major contributions are: Senator John P. East, for the foreword and generous praise of the manuscript; Dr. Otto Butz, who in the strictest definition of the word "Mentor" remains a wise and trusted counselor; and, my wife Nancy, for the immeasurable patience, understanding, and love.

-AHB
May 1984

FOREWORD

Since the late 1960's the Western world has been living in an age of terrorism, an age in which the use of the most brutal violence against seemingly random targets is increasingly regarded as an acceptable means of advancing the political and social goals of the perpetrators. This is especially visible in the so-called "Third World" — the Middle East, Africa, Latin America , and the Far East — but it is by no means unknown in Western Europe and the United States. The counter-culture, the passion for immediate solutions to long-term problems, and the erosion of traditional values and institutions under the impact of modernization are among the causes of this trend of reliance on ideological violence.

Thus far, the United States has escaped the worst effects of the age of terrorism. We have not undergone the disintegration that has afflicted the societies and political cultures of Uruguay, Turkey, Italy, or El Salvador, for example, although all too many Americans have lost their lives to terrorist atrocities directed against them or other targets. Yet, given what we know of the trend of terrorism and the signs that terrorism can actually achieve results for those making use of it, that some states (including the Soviet Union) support and encourage its use, and that some truly frightening techniques of mass destruction are available to terrorists, it would be foolish for the United States to ignore the potential threats and naive to believe that it can't happen here.

Dr. Buckelew's book is a valuable contribution to the public discussion of how the United States can respond to the terrorist threat. The author is not simply content to recount anecdotes or indulge in speculation. His is a serious, well-documented plan for a governmental structure that will meet the threat. It is designed, as he tells us, to be "politically feasible"; it does not sacrifice civil liberties; it involves both the highest level of executive authority as well as the combined skills and resources of many other federal agencies; and it also brings in the talents of the private sector.

This is not necessarily an endorsement of the specifics of Dr. Buckelew's model, but it is an endorsement of his approach and methods. The public discussion of terrorism and the proper means to combat it has often been sidetracked onto other issues, while concrete plans to meet the terrorist threat and provide protection for the lives and rights of Americans have been neglected. After the bombing of the U.S. Capitol Building in November, 1983, after the violence directed against American Marines and diplomats in Lebanon and Kuwait last winter, it is likely that both the Congress and the American people, as well as the executive branch, will be discussing terrorism for some time to come. There is no better place to begin to understand that threat or to begin the discussion than with a thorough reading of Dr. Buckelew's book, which I hope will lead to a national debate and fruitful reforms growing out of his recommendations.

— John P. East
United States Senate

TABLE OF CONTENTS

CHAPTER 1

INTRODUCTION

Background of the Study

In few periods of American history has terrorism not been a factor of some significance in the nation's political, economic, and social life. The United States owes its very existence to urban terrorism and guerrilla warfare. At the turn of the century, the Industrial Workers of the World--the Wobblies--used bombs extensively in their efforts to destroy the capitalist system and usher in a new anarchist "order." Presidents Lincoln, Garfield, McKinley, and Kennedy were assassinated during their terms in office, and attempts have been made against the lives of other chief executives, most recently against President Reagan. The historical record shows a substantial number of lynchings between 1882 and 1964. Many other occurrences of some form of terrorism in American life can also be substantiated. Following every newsworthy assassination attempt, commentators describe the United States as a "violent" society characterized by easy access to instruments of death and destruction.

Neither is there anything new about terrorism in other parts of the world. Most writers concerned with terrorism and low-level conflict begin their analyses with that period of the French Revolution known as the "Terror," one in which some 40,000 lives were sacrificed on the altar of the new order.[1] In fact, however, Robespierre and his colleagues contributed only the word, not the method, for terrorism has been commonplace during mankind's entire history. "From time immemorial, terrorist acts have included assassination, execution, arbitrary imprisonment, mutilation, seizing hostages and slaves, and a wide variety of atrocities that only fiendish minds could devise."[2]

---

[1]Georges Lefebvre, The French Revolution, vol. 2: From 1793 to 1799, trans. by John H. Stewart and James Friguglietti (New York: Columbia University Press, 1964), p. 120.

[2]Edgar O'Ballance, Language of Violence: The Blood Politics of Terrorism (San Rafael, Calif.: Presidio Press, 1979), pp. 1-2.

Because terrorism has been widespread in all periods of history and because a "terrorist" act is singularly difficult to define,[3] it is not readily apparent why extraordinary attention is being devoted to the subject today. The past ten years have witnessed a veritable explosion of both scholarly and media interest in the subject, with literally hundreds of books and articles about terrorism appearing every year. One writer has observed that "the insignificance of terrorism stands in marked contrast to the attention we pay it," coining the expression "terrorist chic."[4] On the other hand, organizations such as the Central Intelligence Agency and the Rand Corporation maintain carefully compiled statistics regarding the incidence of both intranational and international terrorism, numerous scholars investigate the phenomenon, and congressional committees hold hearings trying to find out how to cope with the threat posed by terrorism.

The American journalist Claire Sterling has labeled the last ten years the "Fright Decade" because of the upsurge in terrorism,[5] and there is some substance to that description. While it would be difficult to prove that terrorism is more prevalent today than it was earlier, it is certainly more conspicuous because of the widespread media coverage it receives. Modern communications have made the world a single, well-lit stage. The influence of media coverage on national mood is underscored by the United States' reaction to the recent Iranian detention of 52 Americans for 444 days, in contrast with the much milder response to the seizure of an American intelligence ship, the USS _Pueblo_, by North Korea in 1968. The 83 crew members of the _Pueblo_ were held for nearly a year and tortured by a small Communist nation, but the incident did not turn into one of the great crises of the time. By contrast, television newsman Walter Cronkite maintained a weekly count of the number of days the American hostages in Iran had been held captive, and the American Broadcasting Company aired a nightly news special on "America Held Hostage."[6] This emphasis on a dispute which could not be resolved easily

---

[3]The problem of defining terrorism is considered at length later in this chapter.

[4]Michael Selzer, _Terrorist Chic: An Exploration of Violence in the Seventies_ (New York: Hawthorn Books, 1979), p. 177.

[5]Claire Sterling, _The Terror Network: The Secret War of International Terrorism_ (New York: Holt, Rinehart and Winston and Reader's Digest Press, 1981), p. 308.

[6]Steven R. Weisman, "For America, A Painful Reawakening," _New York Times Magazine_, Special Edition, 1981, p. 117.

resulted in the United States, in effect, holding itself hostage.[7] It was, perhaps, significant that when American television network crews were in Iran, filming the action taking place in front of the American embassy there, the interest of the American public focused intensely on the hostage situation; when the "camera crews were kicked out of Iran, American interest waned."[8]

The same considerations apply to many or most terrorist activities. Attracting media attention is one of the major objectives of many terrorist actions today. The kidnapping of West Berlin mayoral candidate Peter Lorenz by the Baader-Meinhof terrorists was carried out in such a manner as to monopolize German television for a full 72 hours.[9] Terrorist acts which would have escaped world attention as recently as two decades ago now command the front pages of newspapers in numerous world metropolises. More importantly, television crews travel to the site of any important terrorist action as a matter of routine, to show the world exactly what is happening. The mixture of awe and dread which terrorism inspires is no longer limited to a comparatively small audience in the immediate vicinity of the action. Instead, the action affects people around the world. Terrorism may or may not be more widespread than it was before the advent of television, but the average citizen believes that it is. In democratic societies, changing popular perceptions require appropriate governmental responses, intensifying the concern of the American and other Western governments with terrorism.

Equally important is the fact that terrorists are now able to draw on the resources of modern technology, thereby becoming much more powerful and dangerous than they were in former times. Not too long ago, the terrorist depended on crude, homemade explosives, on firebombs, or on weapons available to the general public. Today's terrorist has access to a wide variety of military weapons, including automatic and semiautomatic rifles and pistols (some with silencers), submachine guns, heavy machine guns, portable surface-to-air missiles, light antitank rocket launchers, and surface-to-surface missiles. Articles explaining how to construct nuclear weapons have appeared in a number of periodicals, and well-founded fears have developed that some terrorist group will, one day, succeed in making or otherwise acquiring nuclear devices. (Four nuclear threats

---

[7]A. M. Rosenthal, "America in Captivity: A Preface," New York Times Magazine, Special Edition, 1981, p. 33.

[8]Weisman, p. 117.

[9]Melvin J. Lasky, "Ulrike Meinhof and the Baader-Meinhof Gang," Encounter 44 (June 1975):7-23.

against New York City have already been made.) Equally possible is the future use of germ warfare and chemical agents by skillful terrorists: a tiny droplet of the VX nerve gas developed by the United States Army, for example, would be sufficient to kill an average human being.[10] There are now terrifying weapons in the world's military arsenals, and any of these weapons could find their way to some of the terrorist groups. Furthermore, social dependence on such communal facilities as water supplies, gas and oil pipelines, and bridges makes these facilities potential targets for terrorists, also enhancing the threat which the latter pose to organized society today.

Contemporary terrorists are more dangerous than those of any past period because many terrorist groups receive direct or indirect support from powerful and rich governments-some of them hostile to the United States. During his Senate confirmation hearings, former Secretary of State Alexander Haig accused the Soviet Union of promoting international terrorism around the world.[11] While the semantics of his statement can be and have been questioned, the available evidence seems to support the conclusion that the Soviet Union assists international terrorists in a variety of ways. Terrorists are trained in such nations as Cuba, South Yemen, Czechoslovakia, and East Germany, and in the Soviet Union itself. Arms suitable for terrorist use flow from the Soviet Union to a number of staging areas, from which they are shipped first to various Eastern European countries, then to their ultimate users, including the Provisional Arm of the Irish Republican Army, the Basque separatists, and other European groups. East Germany, Czechoslovakia, and Bulgaria serve as rest-and-recuperation areas for terrorists working in Europe. Cuba operates a clandestine center for the manufacture of passports and identity cards used by European and other terrorists.[12] In view of the high level of control which the Soviet Union

---

[10]Lowell Ponte, "Terrorism's Monstrous New Age," Next 1 (July/August 1980):48-55; "Latest Worry: Terrorists Using High Technology," U.S. News & World Report, 14 March 1977, p. 69.

[11]Bernard Gwertzman, "Haig Says Teheran Will Not Get Arms," New York Times, 29 January 1981, p. 1.

[12]Claire Sterling, "The Terrorist Network," Atlantic Monthly, November 1978, pp. 37-51; Robert Moss, "Terror: A Soviet Export," New York Times Magazine, 2 November 1980, pp. 42-47; Richard F. Staar, "Worldwide Terrorism: The Soviet Union Is at the Bottom of It," Los Angeles Times, 1 May 1981, part II, p. 11; Brian Crozier, ed., Annual of Power and Conflict, 1978-79 (London: Institute for the Study of Conflict, 1979), pp. 1-18.

maintains over Eastern European governments and the Cuban secret service, few of these activities could take place without Soviet approval and assistance.

A number of other nations are also engaged in the enterprise of assisting various international terrorist groups. Uganda stopped being such a nation when its president, Field Marshal Idi Amin Dada, fled the country in 1979 after its invasion by Tanzanian troops. Libya, however, under the rule of Colonel Muammar Qaddafi, has emerged as one of the world's chief supporters of terrorist groups.[13] Qaddafi has provided money, arms, training, and sanctuary to leading terrorist groups in North Africa and the Middle East, Western Europe, and Black Africa, and in areas extending as far east as the Philippines and Thailand.[14] Although only loosely allied with the Soviet Union and ideologically hostile to the United States, Qaddafi has succeeded in purchasing American hardware and expertise on behalf of the world's terrorists.[15]

Well armed, well trained, and well financed, today's terrorist groups are all the more dangerous as a result of the strong links that have formed between them. These links are not necessarily ideological, and the objectives of diverse groups vary greatly. To whatever extent a terrorist "international" exists, it has been forged by training in the same facilities and by the imperative for circumventing joint action by governments opposed to terrorism.[16] So-called "summit" conferences have been held periodically by leaders of outwardly disparate groups. For instance, a July, 1973, "summit" meeting in Tripoli included representatives of the Palestinians, Iran's Liberation Front, the Turkish People's Liberation Army, the Baader-Meinhof Gang, the Irish Republican Army's Provisional Wing, the Tupamaros of Uruguay, and the Japanese Red Brigades.[17] Many instances

[13]Neil C. Livingstone, "Terrorism: The International Connection," _Army_, December 1980, pp. 14-21.

[14]Amos Perlmutter, "Targeting the Real Soviet-Backed Terrorist," _Long Island Newsday_, 16 April 1981, part II, p. 9-F.

[15]Seymour M. Hersh, "The Qaddafi Connection: Part 1," _New York Times Magazine_, 21 June 1981, pp. 52-72; idem, "Exposing the Libyan Link: The Qaddafi Connection, Part 2," _New York Times Magazine_, 28 June 1981, pp. 32-49.

[16]Albert Parry, _Terrorism: From Robespierre to Arafat_ (New York: Vanguard Press, 1976), pp. 537-43; Robert A. Liston, _Terrorism_ (Nashville, Tenn.: Thomas Nelson, 1977), p. 24.

[17]Livingstone, p. 21.

of joint operations by, and mutual assistance between, different terrorist groups have been documented.[18] This increasing unity adds strength to today's terrorist "international."

While terrorism may not be any more widespread now than in earlier periods of history, a number of factors have combined to make it a matter of serious concern to the United States. Some terrorist groups have attacked Americans both at home and abroad, and international terrorism affects the national interests of the United States adversely.

Contrary to the popular perception that terrorism has made little headway in the United States itself, a Rand Corporation survey, of terrorist incidents between 1968 and 1978 resulting in casualties, found that the United States ranked fifth in the world. International terrorist groups have, however, rarely been known to operate in the United States.[19] Outside the United States, American citizens have become favorite terrorist targets. In 1980, for example, there were 278 separate attacks against American diplomats, businessmen, and even tourists abroad. Nearly half of the attacks were against diplomats, and the parts of the world most dangerous for Americans were Latin America and Western Europe.[20]

Terrorist campaigns designed to destabilize allies of the United States are very disruptive. The Basque separatists have made every effort to thwart the establishment and development of democracy in Spain following decades of the dictatorial regime of Generalissimo Francisco Franco.[21] One ally of the United States, Turkey, has been

---

[18]Brian M. Jenkins and J. Johnson, _International Terrorism: A Chronology, 1968-1974_ (Santa Monica, Calif.: Rand Corporation, March 1975); idem, _International Terrorism: A Chronology, 1974 Supplement_ (Santa Monica, Calif.: Rand Corporation, February 1976).

[19]Brian M. Jenkins, _Terrorism in the United States_ (Santa Monica, Calif.: Rand Corporation, May 1980), pp. 2-3.

[20]National Republican Senatorial Committee, "Terrorism Threatens U.S. National Security," _Special Report_, Washington, D.C., May 1981, pp. 1-4.

[21]Stephen Aris, "Terror in the Land of the Basques," _New York Times Magazine_, 4 May 1980, pp. 82-83.

under intense terrorist attack both from the left and from the right.[22] Another ally, Great Britain, expends considerable amounts of time, money, and blood in trying to control the continuing violence in Northern Ireland.[23] United States policy is complicated by the existence of both right-wing and left-wing terrorism in Latin America.

International terrorism is now a major problem for the United States, one that is likely to become even more acute in the years ahead. The United States has been fortunate in experiencing few major terrorist incidents within its own borders. This good fortune, however, is unlikely to continue, for the United States possesses the most extensive network of news media in the entire world, making it the ideal setting for terrorists seeking the greatest possible publicity for their causes. Even with the relatively low prevailing level of domestic terrorism, however, the interests of the United States are being damaged in both the national and the international political domains.

Statement of the Problem

Up to now, the United States has barely been able to cope with domestic terrorism, much less help its friends and allies deal with international terrorism. As in so many other matters, American leadership is essential if reasonable, responsible governments are to survive in those nations under the most intense pressure from terrorist groups.

Illustrating the inadequacy of existing federal mechanisms for dealing with terrorism was the seizure of the Islamic Center and the B'nai B'rith building in Washington, D.C., in January, 1977, by a group of Hanafi Muslims.

> Nobody knew what to do. The F.B.I. had one idea. The D.C. police had another. The Secret Service had a third. If it hadn't been for the Muslim ambassadors, they'd have been chucking bodies out the windows. At one point the D.C. police wanted to assault the [B'nai B'rith] building from above, but they didn't have anybody who knew how to rappel out of a helicopter. The F.B.I. took some D.C. cops to Virginia to practice rappeling. Thank God they didn't have to use them. All they

---

[22]"Can the Turks Unite Against Terror?" _Economist_ (London), 26 July 1980, pp. 45-46.

[23]Richard H. Brown, "Books and Bombs," _Publisher's Weekly_, 23 January 1981, pp. 81-86.

got out of it was a sprained ankle. The chaos was frightening.[24]

The three Muslim ambassadors were able to intervene in what would normally have been a purely domestic matter only because the Hanafi Muslims had also occupied the Islamic Center, the Washington mosque constructed and owned by the Muslim embassies in the nation's capital.

This incident exemplifies much of what has been typical of the American response to terrorism. Jurisdiction in the seizure of the B'nai B'rith building rested primarily with the District of Columbia police, with a strong interest on the part of the Federal Bureau of Investigation. Members of the same Hanafi Muslim group had also seized the Islamic Center, and the State Department was involved in this aspect of the situation because of the interest of the Muslim embassies in Washington. Congress, which exercised considerable powers over the operations of the District government at the time, was also involved, at least in terms of general responsibility. The foreign-policy implications of the mosque's seizure created a presidential interest, even though the record does not show that the White House played an active role in resolving the crisis. The situation illustrated a fragmentation of responsibility, or even a Balkanization, with a number of "sovereign" agencies and departments taking turns in handling the crisis.

The inadequacy of the American response, however, cannot be attributed entirely to fragmentation of responsibility, as the Iranian hostage situation (1979-1981) made clear. News of the Iranian "militants'" attack on the American embassy in Teheran (Tehran) reached Assistant Secretary of State for Near Eastern Affairs Harold H. Saunders by telephone. Before the embassy capitulated, Secretary of State Vance and President Carter had been apprised of the situation. From the very outset, the president of the United States, with the immense resources of his office, was in charge of the crisis. "Fragmentation of responsibility" could not be regarded as the cause of the wavering, the vacillation between tough and conciliatory postures, and the inability to understand that the individuals and groups with whom the United States was making extraordinary efforts to negotiate did not have the power to release the hostages.[25]

[24]Gregory F. Rose, "The Terrorists Are Coming," Politics Today, July/August 1978, p. 52.

[25]Terence Smith, "Putting the Hostages' Lives First," New York Times Magazine, Special Edition, 1981, pp. 77-101.

Various military options were considered immediately after the start of and throughout the long crisis. Even after the humiliation at Desert One, planning for additional military missions continued.[26] Oceans of ink have been used in commenting on the disastrous rescue attempt, but it seems clear that the means employed were simply not adequate to the task. If there were failures in the conception and execution of the rescue attempt, they cannot be attributed to poor coordination within the government of the United States.

Officially, "the rescue attempt collapsed through the mechanical failure of several helicopters before the force could reach Tehran."[27] The failure of a number of helicopters was predictable.

> The length of the flight to Desert One--over 500 miles--the known delicacy of helicopters in flight, the probability that in April the force would encounter dust storms, all point out that the limitation of the force to eight helicopters was a serious misjudgment.[28]

Yitzhak Rabin, former Israeli prime minister and chief of staff, was astonished that the United States deployed such a minimal force in view of the large number of helicopters available to it.[29] The Special Operations Review Group, established to prepare a critique of the operation, indicated that the risk of failure would have been reduced had the number of helicopters used been increased. Under Joint Task Force Combat rules, there should have been at least ten helicopters. Under a "most-likely-case scenario," there should have been at least 11, and if the record of earlier, comparable operations had been consulted, there would have been at least 12.[30] As matters turned out, only five of the helicopters were operational by the time they arrived at Desert One--one fewer than the number considered essential to complete the mission.

---

[26]Drew Middleton, "Going the Military Route," New York Times Magazine, Special Edition, 1981, pp. 103-12.

[27]J. C. Hurewitz, "The Middle East: A Year of Turmoil," in Foreign Affairs: America and the World, 1980, ed. William P. Bundy (New York: Pergamon Press, 1981), p. 549.

[28]Middleton, p. 108.

[29]Ibid.

[30]Ibid., p. 109.

Coordination before and after the Desert One landing, by contrast, can best be categorized as classically thorough. The rescue plan was prepared by military personnel with experience in somewhat similar operations. The CIA provided the planners with the location of Desert One, an airstrip formerly used by Savak (the Shah's secret police force), as well as with details of the Iranian radar installations. The State Department contributed detailed blueprints and descriptions of the embassy buildings and compound so that the commandos would know exactly where to go and what to do. The Army, Air Force, Navy, and Marines were all involved in the planning and operation of the mission. The plans were studied by the Joint Chiefs of Staff and by the National Security Council before being approved by the president. Following the arrival at Desert One, when it became clear that the helicopter force would be inadequate to evacuate troops and hostages, both of the commanders involved recommended that the mission be aborted. They reported their recommendation to a joint task force in Washington, which relayed their message to President Carter through then Secretary of Defense Harold Brown.[31] It therefore seems difficult, if not impossible, to attribute the mission's failure to problems of coordination.

The seizure of the American embassy in Teheran and the holding of 52 American diplomatic, consular, and service personnel for 444 days represents the most serious single failure ever of the United States to deal with international terrorism abroad in a matter affecting national prestige and security. For the nation as a whole, the resulting sense of frustration probably contributed significantly to the eventual repudiation of President Carter at the polls. American prestige abroad certainly suffered. "There was a feeling in this country until the 444th day that it was not just the 52 but all Americans, and worse still, our very Government that had been taken captive and held hostage in that embassy."[32] The incident showed terrorists the world over how easily this particular superpower could be brought to its knees. It has been speculated that the election of President Reagan and the belief that he would pursue a harder line against terrorists may well have saved the United States further embarrassment from groups eager to emulate the Iranian "militants."

Throughout his presidential campaign, Reagan made it clear that he would pursue a hard line against terrorism, which he considered the creature of Soviet expansionism. In his October 19, 1980, televised campaign speech, Reagan said:

---

[31]Ibid., pp. 109-10.

[32]Rosenthal, p. 35.

Let us turn now to the need for the United States
to assume the leadership role in curbing the
spread of international terrorism. In sharing the
outrage against terrorism, I will direct the
resources of my administration against this
scourge of civilization and toward expansion of
our cooperation with other nations combating
terrorism in its many forms.[33]

In the same speech, he called for strengthening the ability
of the CIA and other intelligence agencies to act, and he
also indicated that he would take the lead in "forging an
international consensus that firmness and refusal to concede
or pay ransom are ultimately the only effective deterrents
to terrorism."[34] In commenting on the agreement with Iran
to free the hostages, he indicated reluctant acceptance, but
stated that "the present administration would not have
negotiated with Iran for the release of the hostages. Future
acts of state-sponsored terrorism against the United States
will meet swift and sure punishment."[35] This statement was
consistent with Reagan's posture throughout his campaign.

The two situations just discussed are the two most
striking instances of the inadequacy of existing federal
mechanisms for dealing with national and international
terrorism, but many more examples could be cited.   Politicians today point with pride to the fact that no Americans
are fighting abroad in any declared war.   What they do not
mention, however, is that a significant toll is being taken
of the lives of American diplomats and businessmen and of
American property, in the undeclared war of terrorism
against organized governments and societies.

The problem which this study chose to investigate
was the question of what could be done to place the United
States in a better future position vis-a-vis both domestic
and international terrorism. As the Hanafi takeover
situation showed, the problem is partially of a structural
nature, suggesting the desirability of developing a model
structure including improved governmental mechanisms for
dealing with acts of terrorism. The Iranian experience, on
the other hand, demonstrated deficiencies in intelligence,
contingency planning, advance development of adequate
military forces, national will, and other essential
factors--deficiencies which must also be overcome if the
United States is to deal effectively with future terrorist
acts and situations.

---

[33]Cited in Rowland Evans and Robert Novak, The
Reagan Revolution (New York: E. P. Dutton, 1981), p. 195.

[34]Ibid.

[35]Ibid., p. 196.

Purpose of the Study

This study examines the existing mechanisms of response to terrorist acts against the United States and against certain foreign nations which, unlike the United States, have demonstrated a high level of ability in coping effectively with terrorism. The aim is to develop an improved model of response mechanisms for possible use by the United States.

Importance of the Study

American intelligence agencies are reportedly predicting that international terrorism will gradually change its strategy, perpetrating terrorist acts within the United States itself instead of virtually limiting itself to attacking American personnel and facilities abroad. This expectation is based on the growing number of individuals in the United States potentially or actually sympathetic to terrorist groups. A handful of terrorists can inflict great damage on a society, provided that they have a reasonable base of support in the community, supplying them with safe houses, forged papers, weapons, and explosives. The money needed can be obtained through ordinary criminal acts or from abroad. Terrorist groups in the United States include the Puerto Rican and Croatian nationalists who have already committed terrorist acts and Cubans, Iranians, Palestinians, and others with sympathizers in the United States who have heretofore been relatively inactive. The expectation of intensified domestic terrorism is also based on the improved capabilities of terrorists themselves.

Illustrating the kind of terrorist act that can easily be carried out today was the disaster that struck the city of Newark, New Jersey, on July 7, 1981. Because a valve on the pipeline carrying water to Newark broke or was opened, the city's two major water mains ruptured, spilling some 75 million gallons of water from the city's principal reservoir and cutting off half of the city's regular water supply for at least a month. Just as the summer heat is at its worst, a city which has experienced substantial racial unrest in the past has no water for its swimming pools and other recreational facilities. Official opinions concerning the cause of the rupture differ, and no terrorist or other group has yet claimed "credit" for it.[36] However, state and local officials have confirmed that there was easy access to the concrete blockhouse containing the crucial valves on which the city depends for its water. Any enterprising terrorist group could easily cripple a number of other

---

[36]Robert Drogin, "Newark Is Seeking Additional Water as Mains Burst," Washington Post, 8 July 1981, p. A-8.

American cities in the same way that Newark has been crippled.

The assassination of President John Kennedy and the attempt on the life of President Ronald Reagan demonstrate how easily the best-protected American leader can be attacked. Disputes continue to swirl around the Kennedy assassination. The least to be said about the latter is that law enforcement authorities have failed to make a conclusive case for a lone gunman acting out some irrational impulse. The Kennedy assassination disrupted an entire generation, changed the course of American history, and left a bitter residue of suspicion. The attempted assassination of Reagan, had it succeeded, might have been just as effective in changing the course of history.

The United States, as leader of the free world, needs to demonstrate leadership in combating international terrorism. Turkey is currently so torn by the terrorism of both right and left that it hardly remains a viable ally. Terrorist groups supported originally by Iraq and subsequently by Libya and the Palestinians played a role in the overthrow of the Shah of Iran, the cornerstone of American policy in the Persian Gulf region.[37]   Since the major powers have, for the time being, checkmated each other with their massive nuclear arsenals, the outcome of the continuing struggle between them may well be determined by low-level conflict, of which terrorism is one important aspect.

For the reasons just cited--the likelihood of a sharp increase in terrorist acts within the United States, the major disruptions and disasters that terrorists can visit on American cities, and their ability to change the course of history through assassinations--evolving methods for reducing the incidence of terrorist acts and for coping effectively with such acts of terrorism as do occur is a pursuit of cardinal importance. This study seeks to make a contribution to that pursuit.

Need for the Study

Considerable governmental attention has been devoted to the problem of terrorism in recent years. Both the executive and the legislative branches of government have addressed the problem repeatedly. As the magnitude of the terrorist threat has grown, large numbers of books and articles have appeared on the subject, most of them by journalists. A number of scholars have also written books

---

[37]Walter Laqueur, Terrorism: A Study of National and International Political Violence (Boston: Little, Brown and Co., 1977), p. 211.

and articles on the subject, but have concerned themselves primarily with terrorism abroad.

Because the emergence of the modern-day terrorist threat to the United States is such a recent phenomenon, very few nongovernmental studies of possible improvements in the existing federal response structure have been conducted. Needed urgently is a comprehensive, up-to-the-moment review of the subject, conducted in a scholarly manner and for scholarly reasons, permitting carefully and dispassionately reasoned conclusions and recommendations to be formulated. This study pursues that objective.

Definitions of Terms

As is the case in most comparatively new disciplines or research areas, there is a tendency to resort to a specialized jargon in writing about terrorism, in a sometimes specious attempt to confer credentials of authority and respectability on its user. To the extent possible, such jargon has been avoided in this study. However, the word terrorism itself happens to be one extremely difficult to define. It is, therefore, considered here.

Terrorism. Many of the writers cited earlier in this chapter use the word terrorism loosely, or at least without defining it with any degree of precision. Formidable problems are encountered in formulating a reasonably precise and objective definition of the word.

Part of the problem stems from the fact that terrorism is a pejorative term. If one side to a dispute succeeds in attaching the terrorist label to its adversary, it has gained an important psychological advantage.

This problem can best be illustrated by examining the Arab-Jewish dispute over Palestine and Israel. Before the state of Israel was established, Zionists carried out one of the most elaborate and devastating terrorist campaigns in history. Bombs were placed in cafes, buses, and hotels; there were large numbers of shootings and kidnappings; and numerous letter and parcel bombs were sent to British politicians regarded as being opposed to the creation of the state of Israel. Simultaneously, terrorist campaigns were launched against Arab residents of Palestine in order to induce them to leave. Count Bernadotte, the United Nations mediator, was assassinated by three men believed to be members of the Stern Gang.[38] Members of the

---

[38]O'Ballance, pp. 15-28.

Stern Gang, the Irgun Zvai Leumi, and the Haganah were classified as terrorists by the British government and by most observers not emotionally involved in the struggle for a Jewish state.

Once the state of Israel had been established, it was the displaced Palestinian Arabs fighting for their homeland who became the terrorists as they undertook well-publicized actions against Israel and Israeli nationals. That, at least, is how they are described by the Israeli government and perceived by most Americans. However, a majority of the countries holding membership in the United Nations have condemned Zionism as "a form of racism and racial discrimination,"[39] and the present prime minister of Israel, Menachem Begin, was the leader of the Irgun Zvai Leumi from its formation in 1943 until its dissolution in 1948.[40] It is Begin, the former avowed terrorist, who refuses to negotiate with the present terrorist Yasser Arafat, leader of the Palestine Liberation Organization.

The actions carried out by an individual or a group whose objectives are approved or lauded are not usually considered terrorist by the news media and in public opinion. "Americans, for example, applauded the first two waves of airline hijackings, refugees from the Communist countries of Eastern Europe and then from Cuba."[41] When a group of Afghan rebels assassinates a Soviet officer, its act is not described as terrorist in the Western press. Quite often, the same individual or group may be perceived as terrorist by one side but as heroic by the other.

People generally attach the label of terrorism to some act of violence with whose underlying objectives they do not agree. However, the world is full of situations where one group is pitted against another. Many of the groups so engaged have ethnic or other ties to certain segments of the American public. For many Americans, members of the Provisional Irish Republican Army are heroes; for many more, terrorists.

The Rand Corporation, which has kept an inventory of terrorist incidents for a number of years, believes that an objective definition of terrorism can be formulated. If it were not possible to formulate such a definition, there

---

[39]Parry, p. 449.

[40]Walter Laqueur, ed., The Terrorism Reader: A Historical Anthology (New York: New American Library, 1978), p. 121.

[41]J. Bowyer Bell, A Time of Terror (New York: Basic Books, 1978), p. 96.

could be no chronology of terrorist acts and their analysis would be extremely difficult. The Rand Corporation uses the following criteria:

> Terrorism, in the Rand chronology, is defined by the nature of the act, not by the identity of the perpetrators or the nature of their cause. All terrorist acts are crimes--murder, kidnapping, arson. Many would be violations of the rules of war, if a state of war existed. All involve violence or the threat of violence, often coupled with specific demands. The violence is directed mainly against civilian targets. The motives are political. The actions generally are carried out in a way that will achieve maximum publicity. The perpetrators are usually members of an organized group, and unlike other criminals, they often claim credit for the act. And finally the act is intended to produce effects beyond the immediate physical damage.[42]

The problem created by the Rand definition is clear from the numerous qualifying terms it uses--"many," "often," "mainly," "generally," and "usually." These qualifiers allow for the injection of personal idiosyncrasies in deciding whether a particular act is or is not "terrorist." On the other hand, defining terrorism by focusing on the nature of the act rather than on the identity of the perpetrators or the nature of their cause makes a substantial degree of objectivity possible.

The Rand definition of terrorism implies that governments as well as individuals and groups may be terrorist. However, a survey of the Rand chronologies indicates that very few examples of the use of terror by governments against their own nationals are included. Neither are incidents listed in which terrorists operate within their own nation against their own countrymen. When Irishmen in Northern Ireland kill or otherwise terrorize each other, the incidents are not included in the chronologies; when members of the Irish Republican Army kill Englishmen, the incidents are included.

The Central Intelligence Agency makes a distinction between "transnational terrorism" or terrorism "carried out by basically autonomous nonstate actors, whether or not they enjoy some degree of support from sympathetic states," and

---

[42]Brian M. Jenkins, The Study of Terrorism: Definitional Problems (Santa Monica, Calif.: Rand Corporation, December 1980), pp. 2-3.

"international terrorism," which is terrorism carried out by individuals or groups controlled by a sovereign state.[43] Whether or not a particular terrorist act was financed by a "sympathetic" state or commissioned by a foreign government is usually so difficult to determine that the distinction would seem to be meaningless in the real world. Did Qaddafi "control" or merely "support" "Carlos the Jackal"? If the answer to that question is known, it is so only through using the most sensitive and classified sources and methods and is probably not available to any ordinary scholar.

Attempts by Congress to develop a viable definition of international terrorism have not, thus far, yielded tangible results.[44] For example, section 202 of H.R. 1179, "A Bill to amend the Internal Security Act of 1950 to control and penalize terrorists, and for other purposes," defines "crimes of terrorism" as:

. . . espionage, sabotage, kidnapping, extortion, skyjacking, robbery, bombing, holding a person prisoner or hostage, or any threat or attempt to kidnap, extort, skyjack, bomb, or hold prisoners or hostages, or any threat to do any injury to a human being, animal, or personal or real property or any conspiracy to do any of the above, in order to compel an act or omission by any person, or any governmental entity.[45]

This definition has a drawback: it does not distinguish between common crimes and acts normally regarded as within the realm of international terrorism.

There is a growing but still seriously incomplete body of international law concerning international terrorism. Several conventions dealing with skyjacking have been accepted by those nations carrying the bulk of the world's air passengers and cargo. Forty countries have accepted the Convention on the Prevention and Punishment of Crimes Against Internationally Protected Persons, Including

---

[43]David L. Milbank, International and Transnational Terrorism: Diagnosis and Prognosis (Washington, D.C.: Central Intelligence Agency, April 1976), pp. iii, 9.

[44]Anthony C. E. Quainton, "Statement," in Hearings Before the Subcommittee on Aviation of the Committee on Public Works and Transportation, House of Representatives, 96th Congress, 1st Sess. (Washington, D.C.: Government Printing Office, 28 February 1979).

[45]Cited in E. Nobles Lowe and Harry D. Shargel, eds., Legal and Other Aspects of Terrorism (New York: Practicing Law Institute, 1979), p. 357.

Diplomatic Agents adopted by the United Nations General Assembly on December 14, 1973, but their action has had little practical effect. Attempts by the United States in 1972 and by West Germany in 1976 to have the General Assembly adopt more sweeping provisions against international terrorism failed because "one man's terrorist is another's freedom fighter."[46] Terrorism cannot, therefore, be defined either satisfactorily or comprehensively by referring to relevant international law.

J. Bowyer Bell has said that, "like love, terrorism is easy to recognize but difficult to define."[47] In fact, however, terrorism is no easier to recognize than it is to define.

For the purposes of this study, terrorism is defined as violent, criminal behavior designed primarily to generate fear in the community, or in a substantial segment of the community, for political purposes. When such behavior impinges on the consciousness and concerns of the entire nation, then the nation becomes the community in the definition. Domestic terrorism is such behavior carried out by indigenous population elements. International terrorism is such behavior carried out in the United States by foreign groups or abroad by indigenous population elements. In the context of this study, international terrorism is terrorism designed to affect unfavorably the security interests of the United States. Criminal acts so orchestrated as to threaten the stability and territorial integrity of allies of the United States, thereby affecting adversely the security interests of the United States, are classified as terrorism.

For instance, activities by the Basque separatists intended to secure a measure of autonomy from Spain would not in themselves be considered terrorist acts. When, on the other hand, these activities are designed to destroy the fragile fabric of Spanish democracy so as to encourage the creation of a rightist, totalitarian regime in order to facilitate the ultimate formation of a Marxist government, they become terrorist.

A definition of this kind, while useful for the purposes of this study, would never be adopted by the United Nations, which has held discussions concerning the definitions of terrorism for several years. The definition is

---

[46]Louis G. Fields, Jr., "Terrorism: Summary of Applicable United States and International Law," in Legal and Other Aspects of Terrorism, ed. E. Nobles Lowe and Harry D. Shargel (New York: Practicing Law Institute, 1979), p. 10.

[47]Bell, p. 95.

deliberately "ethnocentric" in that it labels as terrorists all those who use violent, criminal behavior to attack the vital interests of the United States. Neither the Soviet bloc nor most Third World countries would be likely to vote in favor of a definition geared so closely to Western interests. The Soviet Union has an interest in trying to label all individuals and groups working against Western interests in a violent manner as "freedom fighters" participating in "wars of national liberation," not in terrorist acts. Many Third World countries achieved independence as the culmination of an armed struggle which typically began with terrorist acts; they are hardly likely to condemn many of the terrorists operating in the world today. Together, the Soviet bloc and the Third World hold a majority of the votes in the General Assembly, which would be the only body able to endorse a general definition of terrorism for the world organization. A United Nations definition of a threat becomes feasible only when a particular activity, like skyjacking, becomes sufficiently onerous to a majority of the members of the three major blocs in the United Nations. In the case of terrorism, that stage has not yet been reached, judging by the failure of the United Nations General Assembly to agree on a definition of international terrorism. If the time ever comes when there is general agreement that international terrorism must be curbed, any definition adopted will have to be couched in universal, and not in pro-Western, terms.

How to define the national security interests of the United States is a partially subjective question. However, it appears to focus attention where it is needed, on those terrorist acts which affect adversely American power, stability, and security.

Study Questions

This study sets itself, and attempts finding tentative answers to, the following questions:

1. What is the existing federal response structure for dealing with terrorism? That is, how does the United States currently deal with domestic and international terrorism?

2. What are the comparable response structures of other nations?

3. Are there weaknesses in the existing American response structure?

4. What are some of the perceived strengths of the response structures of other nations?

5.   What improvements in the existing federal response structure have been suggested by various knowledgeable individuals?

6.   What can be suggested as the best possible model for the United States to adopt?

Classifying Terrorists: A Conceptual Framework

The United States needs a capacity for coping with a wide variety of terrorist individuals and groups. Terrorists can be classified by type of perpetrator, motive, and kind of action taken.   A brief analysis using actual examples will serve to clarify the conceptual framework of the study.

Type of Perpetrator

The perpetrators of terrorist acts may be lone individuals, small groups, or relatively large organizations such as the Palestine Liberation Organization (PLO) or the Irish Republican Army (IRA).

The lone individual has had a dramatic impact on American history. A major example is that of Lee Harvey Oswald, charged with the assassination of President Kennedy on November 22, 1963, and himself assassinated just two days later by Jack Ruby, a Dallas nightclub owner. The official picture painted of Oswald was that of an alienated and angry man searching for the perfect society and for his own place in history. "His commitment to Marxism and communism appears to have been another factor in his motivation."[48]   If the official version is correct, Oswald was certainly a terrorist, for he committed a violent act, criminal in nature, for political objectives, affecting adversely the security of the United States. Some individuals have argued that Oswald was really part of a larger conspiracy, in which case he would still have been a terrorist, but not a lone perpetrator.   The men who assassinated Senator Robert Kennedy and Dr. Martin Luther King, Jr., and the man who attempted to kill President Reagan, have also been described officially as lone gunmen.

The Fighters for Free Croatia (Ustasha) are an example of a small group which, during the past 50 years, has succeeded in causing considerable carnage. In September, 1976, the group hijacked a Trans World Airlines flight

---

[48]President's Commission on the Assassination of President Kennedy, Report (Washington, D.C.: Government Printing Office, 1964), pp. 423-24.

from New York to Chicago and placed a bomb in a subway locker near the Commodore Hotel on 42nd Street in New York City. It demanded publication of its nationalist ultimata for a free Croatia, with the dropping of its leaflets over New York, Chicago, and Montreal. When the plane landed in Paris, the French shot its tires flat and refused to negotiate with the hijackers. The American ambassador in Paris convinced the group that its demands had been met, whereupon they surrendered and were returned to New York for trial. One New York City police bomb expert was killed and another seriously wounded in disposing of the subway bomb. The particular group that carried out the terrorist operation consisted of five persons, all of whom were on the plane and all of whom were arrested.[49]

One of the largest terrorist groups is a complex of Palestinian organizations, although comparatively few of the militant Palestinian organizations engage in terrorist activities. More than 700,000 Palestinian Arabs fled their homes in 1948, and their numbers have increased naturally over the years since then.[50] A young population, largely loyal to the PLO and determined to return to a country many of them have never seen, they form a large reservoir of manpower for various operations directed against Israel and its friends and interests. Al' Fatah is the military arm of the PLO, with at least 10,000 to 15,000 men under arms at all times, until recently in Lebanon. Most Al' Fatah forces engage in orthodox military operations against Israel and other targets and have recognized that terrorist operations are counterproductive. The majority of Palestinian terrorist operations has been undertaken by Dr. George Habash's Popular Front for the Liberation of Palestine (PFLP), numbering no more than 500 adherents in 1975.[51] In the past, Habash and his organization have been at the heart of the international terrorist movement, using Japanese terrorists to massacre 27 passengers at Lydda Airport in May, 1972.[52] The PFLP was responsible for the kidnapping of

---

[49]Bell, pp. 6-35.

[50]Harry B. Ellis, "The Arab-Israeli Conflict Today," in The United States and the Middle East, ed. Georgiana G. Stevens (New York: American Assembly, Columbia University, 1964), pp. 135-36.

[51]Laqueur, Terrorism, p. 191.

[52]Paul Wilkinson, Political Terrorism (New York: John Wiley and Sons, 1974), p. 123.

the OPEC oil ministers, the hijacking of the French jet airplane to Entebbe, and the bombing of the Istanbul airport in retaliation for the Entebbe rescue mission.[53]

Terrorists must generally operate in small groups for security reasons. Terrorist groups which succeed in disrupting a society may be able to take the next step upward, inaugurating guerrilla warfare, a subject outside the scope of this study. It is very helpful if a terrorist organization has a relatively large population from which to draw its recruits. The IRA, the Basques, and the Palestinians are in this position. Moreover, sizable terrorist bands need a much larger group of sympathizers to provide support and cover if they are to be effective.

Entire governments may also devote themselves to terrorism. This terrorism may be of the right or the left; examples include "Papa Doc's" Haiti and Idi Amin's Uganda in recent times, and Hitler's Germany and Stalin's Soviet Union in the less recent past.[54] There are also governments, including Qaddafi's Libya and Castro's Cuba, which seek to export terrorism with Soviet assistance. Strongly suspected of providing active support for most terrorist governments of the left is the Soviet Union.

Perceived Motives

In some cases, the motives of the perpetrators of terrorist acts are easy to understand, as in the case of the Croatians seeking separation from Yugoslavia.[55] In the case of other separatist or integrationist groups, however, the obvious motive is not always the real one. The Provisional IRA, for example, is not interested merely in separating Northern Ireland from the United Kingdom and uniting it with Catholic Ireland. According to Claire Sterling, the real motive of the Provisional IRA is to destabilize capitalism in the whole of Ireland and in Great Britain as well. The new breed of Basque separatists could have the sort of regional autonomy for which generations of Basque nationalists have fought, but it, too, has placed Marxism above purely Basque interests.

---

[53]Brian M. Jenkins, "International Terrorism: A Balance Sheet," in Contemporary Terrorism: Selected Readings, ed. John D. Elliott and Leslie K. Gibson (Gaithersburg, Md.: International Association of Chiefs of Police, 1978), p. 249.

[54]Parry, pp. 500-501.

[55]Bell, p. 17.

One major motive of terrorists is, therefore, hatred
of Western capitalism and what they view as imperialism.
Terrorist groups may be anarchist, Trotskyite, Maoist, or
orthodox followers of the current Moscow line. Although
their combination may appear extremely unstable, groups with
this kind of political motive are likely to cooperate in
their tactics.

Hatred both of Marxism and of democracy serves as a
motive for right-wing terrorism. For instance, Fascist
groups are believed responsible for a wave of bombings in
France, Italy, Germany, and Spain during the past year.[56]

Ultimately, terrorist groups of both left and right
hope to gain political power as a result of their operations. Realization of this hope may be remote, but there are
a number of contemporary examples (Algeria, Cuba) where
terrorism provided the basis for the development of guerrilla warfare and the ultimate seizure of national power.

Various psychological motives have been ascribed to
terrorists. David Hubbard and F. Gentry Harris have
concluded that most terrorists suffer from some organic
damage which stunts normal interpersonal development. Thus,
a study of 80 imprisoned skyjackers in 11 different
countries discovered that a majority of them suffered from
an impairment of middleear function causing dizziness and
other symptoms. Psychiatrist Adolphe Jonas believes that
terrorists suffer from personality problems attributable to
inconsistent mothering. Terrorists, in this view, experience
a state of dysphoria which can be relieved only by extreme
stimulation, including drug taking, vandalism, cruelty,
suicidal gestures, and terrorism. Most psychologists and
psychiatrists agree that terrorists suffer from some
psychological disorder, but there is little agreement among
them regarding the etiology or nomenclature of the ailment.
Whether or not an individual afflicted with an organic or
psychological ailment of the kind described will turn to
terrorism or to some other activity seems to depend heavily
both on societal conditions and on accidental circumstances.
Brian Jenkins notes that terrorist groups have something in
common with the religious cults now springing up all over
the world--charismatic leaders and a millennialist view of
the world.[57]   The violence perpetrated by the Charles
Manson family and the Jonestown massacre seems to support
this observation.

---

[56]Paul Wilkinson, "Still Working for the Extinction
of Mankind," Across the Board, January 1981, pp. 27-30.

[57]Constance Holden, "Study of Terrorism Emerging as
an International Endeavor," Science 203 (5 January 1979):
33-35.

Two major points merit emphasis. First, political motives cannot necessarily be accepted at face value. The Provisional IRA, for example, claims to want integration with Ireland, but some of its leaders and members really want a Marxist revolution in all of Ireland. Alternatively, some members of this groups may be using a Marxist "cover" in order to continue receiving a large volume of military equipment, training, and financial aid from countries subservient to the Soviet Union. Second, there is no agreement concerning just what constitutes the "terrorist" personality.

Type of Action Taken

Modern terrorists have a wide range of actions available to them, but they have concentrated on a relatively narrow range. The principal types of actions taken are summarized in the following paragraphs.

Aircraft Hijacking. Aircraft hijacking was one of the first innovations of modern terrorism after its adoption by forces inimical to the Soviet Union. Its incidence has been diminished by improved airport security and by international measures to punish the perpetrators.[58] However, as recently as July 10, 1981, two Cuban refugees armed with Molotov cocktails hijacked an Eastern Airlines jet over Florida, forcing it to land in Havana, Cuba. The Cuban government returned the plane to the United States and has promised to deal harshly with the hijackers.[59]

Assassination. The assassination of Archduke Franz Ferdinand on June 28, 1914, at Sarajevo, Bosnia, by a Serbian nationalist student, triggered the First World War. The assassin was one of six students recruited for the action. Earlier in the day, one of the students had tried to kill the archduke with a bomb but missed by a hairsbreadth.[60]

---

[58]P. Clyne, Anatomy of Skyjacking (London: Abelard-Schuman, 1973); A. E. Evans, "Aircraft Hijacking--What Is Being Done?" in International Terrorism and Political Crime (Springfield, Ill.: Charles C. Thomas, 1975), p. 72.

[59]Washington Post, 12 July 1981, p. A-22.

[60]Jere Clemens King, The First World War (New York: Walker and Co., 1972), pp. xxiii-xxv.

The assassination of the key Italian parliamentarian Aldo Moro by members of the Red Brigades was meant to destabilize Italian democracy. Moro was kidnapped on the day that the Italian Chamber of Deputies was due to ratify an agreement among the democratic parties for a new parliamentary majority. Fifty-four days after the kidnapping, Moro's bullet-riddled body was found in a car parked in the center of Rome.[61]

Bombings. Bombs have been used extensively by terrorists, for a variety of purposes. Lord Louis Mountbatten, second cousin of Queen Elizabeth and a war hero, was blown up in his fishing boat off the Irish coast by an explosion set off by a remote-control radio signal. His death by bombing, and that of his grandson and two others, was intended to mark the tenth anniversary of the IRA Provisional Wing's terrorist campaign against the inclusion of Northern Ireland in the United Kingdom.[62] Other bombs, as in the case of the Croatian incident described earlier, are designed to enforce terrorist demands but may take a toll of innocent lives. Bombs are comparatively easy to construct and to conceal, but they can be as lethal to the user as to the target. Books about how to construct homemade explosive devices are readily available in the United States, as are the materials with which to construct them.[63] As already indicated, the possibility that some group may succeed in constructing a nuclear bomb causes genuine concern in security circles.

Extortion. Extortion is used frequently by terrorist groups to obtain money or to secure the release of imprisoned members of such a group. Various methods are used to make this threat credible.[64]

---

[61]Pellegrino Nazzaro, "Order or Chaos in Italy?" Current History 77 (November 1979):172-74.

[62]Bernard Gavzer, "Could His Life Have Been Saved?" Washington Post Parade, 12 July 1981, pp. 14-15.

[63]Each issue of the Shotgun News carries advertisements by publishers such as Paladin Press and Desert Publications, offering books of this sort. The Poor Man's Armorer is a magazine of improvised weaponry which shows the reader how to make a "homemade guided missile."

[64]P. D. Shaw, "Extortion Threats--Analytic Techniques and Resources," Assets Protection 1 (Summer 1975):5-16.

Hostage Taking. Taking and holding hostages is a favorite terrorist tactic, serving a number of purposes. Hostages can be taken to protect the terrorists during the commission of a criminal act, as during a bank holdup to secure money. Hostages can be used as bargaining counters to secure terrorist demands, including the release of political prisoners or the dissemination of political demands as in the Croatian hijacking case. There have been literally hundreds of hostage situations involving terrorists in the past two decades.[65] The hostage situation producing the most farreaching consequences was the holding of the American diplomatic and service personnel in Iran for 444 days.

Kidnapping. Kidnapping is similar to hostage taking, except that the kidnap victim(s) is spirited away and hidden. In Italy and in Latin America, terrorists commonly kidnap prominent persons in order to raise money for their other activities and to undermine the nation's social and economic stability. If the kidnapping has a purely monetary objective, without political overtones, it cannot be considered a terrorist act.

Media Manipulation. Since one of the primary purposes of modern terrorism is to use the news media for its own goals, criminal activities are generally linked to demands for media coverage of the event. The Croatian nationalists demanded that their communique be published in various major newspapers (New York Times, Los Angeles Times, Chicago Tribune, International Herald Tribune, and Washington Post) and dropped by leaflet over Montreal, New York, and Chicago.[66] In other situations, such as the Iran hostage crisis, terrorists are easily able to manipulate the media because they are a major source of news.

Sabotage. Sabotage is a threat against property and populations that has rarely been used by terrorists, so far as is known. The potential for sabotage of such facets of the economy as water supplies and nuclear power plants is so

---

[65]U.S., Department of Justice, Hostage Situations (Quantico, Va.: Federal Bureau of Investigation Academy, January 1975). This bibliography includes more than 400 entries dealing with hostage situations, and there have been many more since 1975.

[66]Bell, pp. 11 and 20.

great, however, that sabotage is usually included in the
relevant literature as a terrorist weapon.[67]

Violence. All terrorist actions are violent, but
the objectives of terrorism generally run counter to killing
large numbers of innocent people.

> Mass murder or indiscriminate violence is contrary
> to the principle of terrorism; terrorists want a
> lot of people watching, not a lot of people dead,
> and killing a few will often suffice. It is
> immoral to kill the "little people" who are not
> the terrorists' enemies.[68]

However, there comes a point where traditional tactics do
not work, the public becomes bored and jaded, and more
Draconian measures must be taken to achieve an impact.
Terrorists may then turn to indiscriminate violence, as in
the bombing of a train station in Bologna, Italy, in which
83 persons were killed and 160 injured.

Assumptions

Four principal assumptions underlie this study:

1. Terrorism will continue to constitute a major
problem for democratic governments throughout the world for
many years to come.

2. Because the public has become accustomed to
terrorist atrocities (such as the attempted assassinations
of President Reagan and of Pope John Paul II and the
American embassy takeover), terrorists will have to increase
the stakes by planning and attempting to execute ever more
daring acts.

3. A dispassionate look at the antiterrorist
strategies and tactics undertaken by various governments is
capable of pinpointing trends, mistakes, lacunae, and
accomplishments which may not be readily apparent to
individuals in operating agencies who must concentrate on
day-to-day developments.

4. The conclusions and recommendations presented
can help enhance the ability of the United States to cope
with terrorism.

---

[67]C. Wilson, The Tupamaros: The Unmentionables
(Boston: Branden Press, 1974).

[68]Brian M. Jenkins, Terrorism in the 1980s (Santa
Monica, Calif.: Rand Corporation, December 1980), p. 5.

Delimitations of the Study

Many important aspects of terrorism have not been covered in this study. The extent to which international terrorism is directly or indirectly controlled by the Soviet KGB (State Security Committee) is outside the scope of the study. The study is limited to the relatively narrow aspects of the existing response mechanisms of the United States and of those countries which have demonstrated an outstanding ability to cope effectively with terrorism.

One obvious tactic or strategy for dealing with terrorism is to give terrorists enough of what they want to isolate them from their sympathizers and supporters. For example, the Basques in France have rarely conducted terrorist activities against the French government because they have traditionally had the right to learn their language, broadcast and publish in Basque, and elect their own candidates to local and national offices. In Spain, where almost all Basque terrorism takes place, the Basques were repressed during the four decades of the Franco regime. Political solutions would definitely alleviate some terrorist pressures. However, it was beyond the space limitations of this study to examine each major terrorist situation in enough detail to lay the foundation for useful suggestions concerning how to deal with each politically. At the same time, the need for political solutions cannot be overlooked entirely. On the other hand, terrorist activities with the ultimate objective of overthrowing the government(s) of the United States or of nations friendly to the United States cannot be diminished by making political concessions to the terrorists. For instance, nothing short of the total destruction of Israel is likely to satisfy the Palestinian terrorists--a "solution" unacceptable to the United States.

Considerable domestic terrorism was generated as a reaction to American involvement in the Vietnam War. Despite the current problems in Central America, the United States is consequently hardly likely to engage in a major conflict there requiring conscription, without a congressional declaration of war. Terrorism in the aftermath of Vietnam is therefore considered only briefly, and the Central American situation not at all. An extended discussion of the subject would also have to take into account officially sanctioned United States government terrorism during the Vietnam period and would serve no useful purpose for this study.

The other major source of "terrorism" in the United States has been the racial situation. The race riots of the 1960's are also considered only briefly, not because they cannot recur, possibly on a greatly magnified scale, but because, in the main, they were not examples of terrorism as the word is defined in this study. The mass outpouring of frustrations typical of most race riots is not political in purpose as much as it is a plea for economic improvement.

CHAPTER 2

THE STRUCTURE AND FUNCTIONING OF U.S. AND SELECTED

FOREIGN RESPONSE MECHANISMS TO TERRORISM

Introduction

The purpose of this study is to examine the existing mechanisms for response to terrorism that have been developed in the United States and in other nations which have demonstrated a consistent ability to cope effectively with terrorism. The goal of the study is to develop an improved model for possible use by the United States.

The following review first considers the terrorism response structure of the United States under Presidents Nixon, Ford, Carter, and Reagan. This is followed by an evaluation of the existing federal response structure, independent of any particular administration. A third section of this chapter examines suggested improvements in the existing federal response structure. The chapter concludes with a survey of the response structures of a number of foreign nations, focusing on their superior elements.

Two preliminary observations are needed to lay the groundwork for a discussion of response mechanisms. To begin with, the term response structure has been defined as the predetermined organizational structure to be used by a government whenever a terrorist act against it takes place. The response structure attempts to define before the event occurs who does what, when, where, and by what authority. Response mechanisms are not, however, by themselves a complete answer to dealing effectively with terrorism. Policies toward sensitive international issues can affect the origin and incidence of terrorist attacks. For example, Palestine's militant Arab groups constitute one of the principal magnetic poles of international terrorism, with ties to many of the world's other terrorist organizations.[1] Recently, former Presidents Ford and Carter both expressed the opinion that the United States ought to enter into

---

[1]Claire Sterling, The Terror Network: The Secret War of International Terrorism (New York: Holt, Rinehart and Winston and Reader's Digest Press, 1981), pp. 272-85.

direct negotiations with the Palestine Liberation Organization as a necessary prelude to establishing a lasting peace in the Middle East.[2] Such a move might well reduce the level of cooperation between Palestinian terrorists and terrorist groups in other areas attacking American interests directly or indirectly.

Another example is provided by the recent revival of terrorist attacks against United States military installations in Germany.[3] These attacks were launched by the Red Army Faction, quiescent for about three years but apparently given a new lease on life by the Reagan administration's decision to manufacture neutron bombs with a view to their eventual use in protecting Western Europe.

> A central difficulty for the Red Army Faction, West German authorities believe, has been its inability to convince any group whose sympathies it hoped to win . . . that its actions represented their interests or could advance their goals. Now the terrorists obviously regard concern in West Germany about new nuclear missiles and the neutron weapon . . . as an ideally sympathetic backdrop.[4]

The terrorist attacks have come against a background of German popular protest against the stationing of new nuclear missiles in that country and the American decision to stockpile neutron bombs.

These examples are only two of the many that could be cited in support of the close links between foreign and military policy and the incidence of terrorism. Major foreign-policy decisions are taken in accordance with overall national interests, without regard to the susceptibilities of comparatively small groups opposed to such decisions, but they can have a considerable impact on the incidence and targets of terrorism.

Secondly, American presidents are both prisoners and spokesmen of their epochs. They are not entirely free to choose courses of action because of constraints placed on them by reactions to the policies of preceding administrations. In domestic affairs, "history informs us that dogmas of the Right breed counterdogmas of the Left; that the

---

[2]Haynes Johnson, "Ford, Carter Unite on Mideast," Washington Post, 12 October 1981, pp. A-1, A-3.

[3]John Vinocur, "German Terrorists Pursue Fresh Targets with Old Strategies," New York Times, 20 September 1981, p. E-3.

[4]Ibid.

dismantling of society's support of the disadvantaged will increase social tensions to the point of violence."[5] In foreign affairs, the Carter administration inherited the post-Vietnam wisdom that "American power . . . was not a last resort' that got you out of trouble; American power was, in fact, what got you into trouble."[6] An inevitable reaction then developed:

> Late last year and early this one [1979], a grim sequence of events seemed to create a sense of what newsmagazines quickly labeled "America in Retreat." Revolution in Iran, withdrawal from Taiwan, war in the Yemens, war (once again) in Vietnam, a Communist coup and then assassination in Afghanistan, near anarchy in Turkey, price buccaneering by OPEC, mercenary militarism on Cuba's part in Africa, and, perhaps most symbolic, gaucherie and rebuke in Mexico.[7]

In 1964, the Gulf of Tonkin Resolution, which had the effect of a congressional declaration of war, was adopted overwhelmingly by the Congress after only a few hours of cursory consideration. The consequences of that action were of such magnitude that a natural reaction to them set in after the Vietnam conflict ended. By the end of 1979, there were more than 150 statutory limitations on United States relations with foreign countries.[8] A far more assertive Congress was one of the consequences of a supine Congress 15 years earlier. Even if President Carter had wished to intervene to block the Cuban excursion into Angola, Congress had the power and the inclination to compel inaction on his part.

The process appears to be a constantly swinging pendulum where extremes dominate. Presidents are not always able to adopt a course of action they consider ideal--to achieve a synthesis out of thesis and antithesis--because public opinion has swung to one extreme or another as a result of previous mistakes or disasters. In considering the measures taken by recent administrations to combat terrorism, it would be a mistake to assume that each president and the members of his administration necessarily did what they considered ideal in the struggle against terrorism.

---

[5]Marshall D. Shulman, "Man Bites Dogma," Columbia, October 1981, p. 18.

[6]Ben J. Wattenberg, "It's Time to Stop America's Retreat," New York Times Magazine, 22 July 1979, p. 14.

[7]Ibid.

[8]William D. Rogers, "Who's in Charge of Foreign Policy?" New York Times Magazine, 9 September 1979, p. 47.

The Federal Response Structure

This section considers in detail the federal response structure as it has evolved during the past four administrations. The review begins with the administration of President Richard M. Nixon (January, 1969--August, 1974).

The Nixon Administration

President Nixon took office on the threshold of the "Fright Decade," as various writers have labeled the 1970's. Although international terrorism was not yet perceived as a serious international problem in 1969, the United States itself had passed through a period marked by internal dissension and violence. Such important pieces of legislation as the Economic Opportunity Act of 1964, the Civil Rights Act of 1964, and the Voting Rights Act of 1965 were designed to combat poverty and make it possible for minorities to participate more actively in American political life. Yet, they had the paradoxical effect of increasing both expectations and militancy on the part of those groups the measures were designed to help.[9] The Watts riot of 1965 was imitated in a number of other major cities, before the urban violence ended somewhat abruptly in 1969.[10] Toward the end of 1966, the war on poverty began to take a back seat to the escalating war in Vietnam. This conflict radicalized a significant segment of the American population and spawned considerable violence.[11]

A large number of radical organizations in the United States engaged in sporadic terrorism during the period from 1965 to 1975. Prominent among them were the Black Muslims, held responsible for the random killing of 14 whites in San Francisco and for a number of shootouts with the police. Several Black Panthers were convicted of plans to bomb various department stores. The Weather Underground organization bombed a New York City police station, while the Students for a Democratic Society occupied Columbia University in 1968. The Symbionese Liberation Army killed Oakland (California) school superintendent Marcus Foster,

---

[9]Theodore Caplow, Sociology, 2nd ed. (Englewood Cliffs, N.J.: Prentice-Hall, 1975), p. 218.

[10]Ibid., p. 331.

[11]Ibid., p. 218.

and later gained nationwide attention by kidnapping heiress
Patricia Hearst.[12] A complete list of terrorist organizations and incidents in the United States during the
1965-1975 period would take many pages.   .

The country was jolted by violence almost continuously from the mid-1960's until the accession of Richard
Nixon to the presidency. Bombings were carried out by such
American revolutionary groups as the Weather Underground,
usually without loss of life, and by such political organizations as the Puerto Rican nationalists, often with loss of
life. Political assassinations took a toll of the lives of
policemen and other public figures.   There were many
disorders, including race riots and hostage situations.[13]

In his series of books on American electoral campaigns, Theodore White wrote of the violence and terror
gripping the nation in 1968:

. . . The marvel of American politics previously
had been its ability to channel passions into a
peaceful choice of directions. In 1968, hate
burst out of the channel, and hate, whether from
student ideologues, unabashed white racists or
black extremists, incubated further hate, loosing
lunatics, gunmen, rock-throwers and club-
wielders.[14]

Candidate Nixon responded to the public's concern
over the widespread violence in his speech accepting the
Republican nomination. He spoke of an America in which
"cities [are] enveloped in smoke and flame. We hear sirens
in the night."[15] For a quiet majority of Americans, the
situation was intolerable. Nixon pledged to eliminate one
of the major problems of the United States by bringing an
"honorable" end to the Vietnam War.[16]   Abroad, "for five
years hardly a day has gone by when we haven't read or heard
a report of the American flag being spit on, and our embassy

---

[12]Marcia McKnight Trick, "Chronology of Terroristic,
Quasi-Terroristic, and Political Violence in the United
States: January 1965 to March 1976," in Disorders and
Terrorism: Report of the Task Force on Disorders and
Terrorism (Washington, D.C.: National Advisory Committee on
Criminal Justice Standards and Goals, 1976), pp. 517-21.

[13]Ibid., pp. 508-17.

[14]Theodore H. White, The Making of the President,
1968 (New York: Atheneum Publishers, 1969), p. xi.

[15]Ibid., p. 254.

[16]Ibid., p. 255.

being stoned, a library being burned, or an ambassador being insulted. . . ."[17] The way to end the terror and humiliations was to reestablish law and order at home, the Republican nominee said. He promised a new attorney general and a new Department of Justice that would make war on criminals and terrorists. Law and order became the theme of his address, one applauded vigorously by the members of the convention.

As if to underline the magnitude of the problem, the 1968 Democratic Convention in Chicago was marred by clashes between demonstrators and police, culminating in the unauthorized police raid on Senator Eugene McCarthy's student supporters at the Chicago Hilton.[18] Another sign of the times was the assassination of Senator Robert Kennedy by Sirhan Sirhan, in June, 1968.

Nixon emphasized the "law and order" issue both in his campaign for nomination and during the election campaign itself. He spoke about uniting the country, terminating the violence at home, and without specifying how, ending the Vietnam conflict.[19] As his opponent, Vice President Hubert Humphrey, began to rise in the polls, Nixon increased his stress on this issue. A major theme of his first inaugural address was the need "to lower our voices,"[20] as a prelude to eliminating the hatred and violence abroad in the land.

One of the Nixon administration's first actions in the campaign against domestic terrorism was revealed only in the later stages of the Watergate crisis. This action involved highly classified, controversial, and far-reaching domestic surveillance of suspected radicals and dissidents.

The so-called Huston plan was a series of national security proposals presented to President Nixon in July, 1970, and approved by him with only minor modifications. Although opposed by the FBI, the plan was actually implemented. Key elements of the plan included: (1) employment of the National Security Agency to cover the communications of American citizens using international facilities; (2) intensified electronic surveillance and penetration of individuals and groups in the United States "who pose a major threat to internal security"; (3) expansion of mail coverage to include targets of priority foreign intelligence

---

[17]Ibid.

[18]Ibid., p. 303.

[19]Ibid., p. 325.

[20]Raymond Price, With Nixon New York: (Viking Press, 1977), p. 379. The author was Nixon's top speech writer during all of his White House years.

and internal security interest; (4) surreptitious entry to permit obtaining vitally needed foreign cryptographic material and other urgent security targets; (5) relaxation of restrictions on the development of campus sources to expand coverage of violenceprone campus and student-related groups; (6) unrestricted expansion of CIA activities overseas with respect to American citizens suspected of ties with domestic radicals and dissidents; and (7) creation of an interagency committee made up of the organizations involved, plus the Defense Intelligence Agency and the military counterintelligence agencies, to provide evaluation of the domestic dissident and terrorist scenes.[21] The classification of the Huston plan was Top Secret, to be handled via Comint (Communications Intelligence) channels only.

The Huston memorandum was approved by President Nixon on July 14, 1970. The only deletions concerned establishing an interagency committee and other implementing measures. The major purpose of these deletions was to minimize the risk that the new measures would come to the attention of Congress and the media.[22]

The "Decision Memorandum" from the White House, also drafted by Huston following approval by the president, made the following points: (1) National Security Council Intelligence Directive Number 6 was to be interpreted to permit the National Security Agency (NSA) to cover American citizens using international facilities such as Telex; (2) the intelligence community was to use electronic surveillance and penetration to intensify coverage of individuals and groups in the United States regarded as a major threat to internal security and of foreign nationals and diplomatic establishments; (3) restrictions on legal mail coverage were to be removed and restrictions on covert coverage were to be relaxed to include mail surveillance of priority foreign intelligence and internal security targets; (4) restraints on the use of surreptitious entry were to be removed insofar as foreign cryptographic and other urgent and high-priority internal security targets were concerned; (5) coverage of violence-prone campus and student-related groups was to be increased; and (6) the CIA was ordered to step up its efforts to penetrate and report on similar groups operating abroad. The memorandum concluded that the president wished

---

[21]Tom Charles Huston, "Operational Restraints on Intelligence Collection," in Big Brother and the Holding Company: The World Behind Watergate (Palo Alto, Calif.: Ramparts Press, 1974), pp. 321-25.

[22]H. R. Haldeman, "Memorandum to Huston: Domestic Intelligence Review, July 14, 1970," Top Secret, in ibid., p. 326.

to have all possible procedural problems that might arise resolved "with maximum speed and minimum misunderstanding."[23]

The "Decision Memorandum" was recalled by the White House as a result of objections by FBI Director J. Edgar Hoover, but it was never technically rescinded and was, in fact, implemented. A memorandum from the president's counsel, John Dean III, to the attorney general demonstrates the eclectic but sweeping approach to domestic intelligence gathering soon adopted by the Nixon administration:

> . . . I believe we agreed that it would be inappropriate to have any blanket removal of restrictions [on the gathering of intelligence by covert means]; rather, the most appropriate procedure would be to decide on the type of intelligence we need, based on an assessment of the recommendations of this unit, and then to proceed to remove the restraints as necessary to obtain such intelligence.[24]

Measures such as these were invoked against a variety of "black power" and antiwar groups, some of which could well be described as domestic terrorist organizations.

Considered particularly dangerous by the Nixon administration were the Black Panthers. On May 11, 1970, J. Edgar Hoover proposed a "disruptive-disinformation operation" against the Black Panthers. The key element of his plan was the fabrication of FBI and police documents to be provided to the Panthers by a "disgruntled" law enforcement employee (an agent provocateur). According to Hoover:

> Effective implementation of this proposal logically could not help but disrupt and confuse Panther activities. Even if they were to suspect FBI or police involvement, they would be unable to ignore factual material brought to their attention through this channel. The operation would afford us a continuing means to furnish the Panther leadership true information which it is in our interest they know and disinformation which, in their interest, they may not ignore.[25]

---

[23]Tom Charles Huston, "Decision Memorandum, July 15, 1970," in ibid., pp. 327-28.

[24]John Dean, "Memorandum for the Attorney General, September 18, 1970," in ibid., p. 329.

[25]J. Edgar Hoover, "Memorandum from the Director of the FBI: FBI Disruption of the Black Panthers, May 11, 1970," in ibid., pp. 317-19.

A special "Panther Squad" was created by the Department of Justice to bring in indictments against members of the organization. Its leadership was jailed, and a number of Panther headquarters around the country were raided or stormed, with some loss of life. Although some FBI and local police officials were subsequently found guilty of crimes and provocations, the Black Panthers were effectively destroyed as a functioning organization.[26]

The machinery created by the Huston plan was also used against the antiwar movement, with less evident success. The movement was too large and amorphous to be destroyed as the Black Panthers had been. Some members of the antiwar movement almost certainly engaged in terrorist actions such as bombings, but the large body of the group was simply exercising the right of free speech.[27]

On June 13, 1971, the New York Times printed the first part of a top-secret history of the Vietnam War, ushering in a still more frenetic attempt to gather domestic intelligence by any means. Daniel Ellsberg was indicted on counts of theft of government property and unauthorized possession of documents and writings related to national defense. Howard Hunt was then hired as a consultant assigned to Charles Colson of the White House staff, to coordinate domestic intelligence and implement exceptionally sensitive (mainly illegal) domestic intelligence operations. Colson, Hunt, and others set in motion the chain of events leading to the illegal break-in at the office of Dr. Fielding, Ellsberg's psychiatrist. The purpose of the operation against Ellsberg was not merely to bolster the case against him, but also to identify his associates and supporters of "the New Left with this negative image."[28] Ellsberg was recognized not to be a terrorist, but some of his associates and supporters were suspect, given the mood of the White House at the time.

The operation against Ellsberg was followed by others directed against various political opponents of the administration, including the Democratic Party, and organized and supervised by the White House itself. These abuses eventually led to the Watergate scandal and Nixon's unprecedented resignation from the presidency.

---

[26]Steve Weissman, "Crying Wolf at Watergate," in ibid., p. 30.

[27]Ibid., pp. 31-34.

[28]New York Times, ed., The Watergate Hearings: Break-In and Cover-Up (New York: Viking Press, 1973), pp. 67-70.

A desire to pursue a hard line against domestic dissidents who dared break the law was expressed publicly on various occasions. Nixon's "law and order" task force recommended the appointment of stricter judges, the use of more wiretaps, the employment of "space-age techniques and hardware," and the training of local police in tactics and the use of equipment. The new president used his first press conference to endorse preventive detention. His attorney general, John Mitchell, called for "no knock" entry, wiretaps, and federal troops to fight crime in the District of Columbia. Mitchell also declared that the Department of Justice would prosecute hard-core militants who crossed state lines to incite riots on campuses and in cities. Deputy Attorney General Kleindienst stated that the Department of Justice was going to crack down on draft dodgers, anarchists, and militants of all radical persuasions. All those who demonstrated in such a manner as to interfere with the rights of others "should be put in a detention camp," Kleindienst told the nation.[29]

There is no evidence to suggest that those Draconian measures, some of them illegal and subsequently resulting in the disgrace or imprisonment of a number of high officials, were particularly effective in curbing domestic terrorism. The Black Panthers were decimated, but it was not entirely clear whether they actually contemplated terrorism or self-defense. Members of the Weather Underground claimed responsibility for 45 bombings between 1970 and 1977, and they have recently started appearing in headlines again.[30] The New World Liberation Front claimed responsibility for 70 bombings in the San Francisco Bay area between 1974 and 1978, and may have been responsible for a large number of additional bombings elsewhere in California and in other western states. The Red Guerrilla Family and the Symbionese Liberation Army remained active through and beyond the Nixon years (1978). The same observations can be made about the George Jackson Brigade and the Sam Melville--Jonathan Jackson Unit; the latter carried out its most recent bombing in February, 1979.[31]

Improvements in the political climate, rather than tactics, appear to have been responsible for the great diminution in domestic terrorism in the United States. "The American withdrawal from Vietnam removed the principal cause of domestic strife. No current issue has the same clarity, urgency, or apparent justification for violence, as did the

---

[29]Weissman, pp. 29-30.

[30]Brian M. Jenkins, Terrorism in the United States (Santa Monica, Calif.: Rand Corporation, May 1980), p. 9.

[31]Ibid., p. 10.

war."[32]   Other issues remain, of course--the economy,
nuclear energy, and certain foreign-policy issues--but they
do not appear to generate the same hostility within a large
segment of the politically active population that the
Vietnam conflict did. During Nixon's first term, the
Vietnam issue was particularly divisive since Nixon had
campaigned on a pledge to end the war with honor. When the
war continued dragging on, fury increased among a number of
individuals and groups.

Part of the problem with the Nixon campaign against
domestic terrorism may have been the self-serving choice of
targets. The White House displayed "a morbid fear of
dissent and, simultaneously, a passion for political
intelligence and an insensitivity to the legal and constitutional restraints on the Presidency on the part of the White
House staff, from top to bottom, and on the part of Nixon
himself."[33]   Instead of taking aim at specific terrorist
targets, the Nixon administration conducted intelligence
operations and campaigns of harassment against a wide range
of dissenters and political enemies. Insensitivity to the
legal and constitutional restraints on the presidency and
the self-serving choice of targets not only brought the
administration down at the climax of the Watergate crisis
but also set back the war against domestic terrorists.

The Nixon administration's efforts to combat
international terrorism were less controversial. Although
terrorism generally existed at a high level during the first
two years of the Nixon administration, the most dramatic
single incident was the assassination of 11 members of the
Israeli team at the 1972 Munich Olympics. Eight members of
a Palestinian faction (the BSO) perpetrated the attack on
September 5, 1972; five were killed by West German police,
while the three who were captured alive were released
several weeks later when a West German airliner was hijacked
by other members of the group. This incident was instrumen-
tal in rousing the United States to shore up its defenses
against international terrorism.[34]

In September, 1972, following the Munich incident,
President Nixon asked the secretary of state to chair a
cabinet committee to consider "the most effective means to

---

[32]Ibid.

[33]R. W. Apple, Jr., in New York Times, ed., The
Watergate Hearings: Break-In and Cover-Up (New York: Viking
Press, 1973), p. 61.

[34]Lewis Hoffacker, "Statement," in Terrorism, Part
2, Hearings Before the Committee on Internal Security, House
of Representatives, 93rd Congress, 2nd Sess. (Washington,
D.C.: Government Printing Office, 1974), p. 3133.

prevent terrorism here and abroad." Included on the committee were the secretary of state as chairman, the secretaries of Treasury, Defense, and Transportation, the attorney general, the American ambassador to the United Nations, the director of the FBI, the director of the Central Intelligence Agency, and the presidential assistants for national security and domestic affairs. (The latter were Henry Kissinger, national security assistant, and Robert Cole, head of the Domestic Affairs Council).[35]

The cabinet committee met at the president's direction shortly after the Munich incident, but very rarely thereafter. Day-to-day operations were delegated to a working group of the cabinet committee under the chairmanship of Ambassador Lewis Hoffacker, special assistant to the secretary of state and coordinator for combating terrorism. This working group met as required by events, not on a regular basis. In practice, it concentrated on problems involving the protection of Americans abroad and of foreign diplomats in the United States.[36]

One of the functions of the working group, operating on behalf of the cabinet committee, was to monitor the implementation of Public Law 92-539, which gave the FBI concurrent jurisdiction with local agencies in protecting foreign officials and official guests. In the event of problems in implementing the law, working group members would request that their principals take appropriate measures to have the law changed or clarified. No such changes were, however, made during the Nixon administration. In cases not involving foreign officials or official guests, the working group would have no function with respect to terrorist actions within the United States.

On the other hand, all incidents involving Americans--both private and official--overseas fell within the purview of the group. Overseas terrorist incidents were normally handled by ad hoc task forces, chaired by Ambassador Hoffacker or Security Chief G. Marvin Gentile, and including State Department desk officers, CIA country specialists, and a news media officer. Task forces varied greatly, depending on the nature and scope of the terrorist incident. In general, anyone with particular expertise required by the task force would be co-opted by the group. Psychiatrists from both the State Department and the CIA would be available as needed, as would be intelligence and country specialists. One informal group was established in 1974 under the formal leadership of Ambassador Hoffacker, to follow the problem of kidnappings of American oilmen in

[35]Ibid., p. 3134.

[36]Ibid., p. 3135.

Ethiopia. Where important incidents were involved, the assistant secretary of state for the area would follow developments in person as chairman of the group under the general authority of Hoffacker. Task forces were usually dismantled when the terrorist incident or problem was resolved one way or another.[37]

Task forces might also be established in cases involving American interests, even where no Americans were directly involved. This procedure was followed partly for "academic" reasons--in order to learn as much as possible about terrorism in general--and partly for normal foreign-policy reasons.[38]

Even with the establishment of the cabinet committee and the working group, there was no unified command in situations with international repercussions. In cases involving foreign diplomats, the FBI would establish its own operations center and would have primary responsibility for any actions taken. Legislation provided the FBI with primary authority to handle the protection of foreign diplomats in the United States. The job of the working group would then be to provide advice and assistance:

> . . . If any foreign affairs become involved, something involving State Department or foreign relations, we are there for advice. The White House would be the ultimate authority there. You have the Secretary of State and the Attorney General focusing on the White House. When you get into foreign affairs, you have to marry it to the domestic.[39]

In other words, despite the level of representation and the scope of its membership, the working group had no command function in domestic terrorist situations with foreign-policy overtones. In terrorist cases involving American interests or nationals overseas, the nation in which the incident occurred would have responsibility for handling matters. The working group could transmit its views and requests to the government concerned through the local embassy or consulate, but had no authority insofar as actions were concerned.

In the field of foreign terrorism, the State Department had various other functions. Americans traveling abroad could obtain advice and information on terrorism and how to cope with it from the country desk at the State

---

[37]Ibid., pp. 3146-47.

[38]Ibid., p. 3148.

[39]Ibid., p. 3140.

Department in Washington. In the field, information would
be obtained from the appropriate officer at the nearest
embassy or consulate. The State Department was also responsible for pressing for ratification by foreign governments
of the three multilateral conventions dealing with hijacking: (1) the 1963 Tokyo Convention requiring nations to
return planes and passengers when a hijacking had taken
place; (2) the 1970 Hague Convention calling on countries
either to extradite or to prosecute hijackers; and (3) the
1971 Montreal Convention specifying that any sabotage of
aviation, such as blowing up planes on the ground, be dealt
with by prosecution or extradition of the offenders. In
addition, the State Department, through the United States
mission to the United Nations, attempted on a number of
occasions to have the United Nations adopt stronger measures
against terrorism. In December, 1973, the General Assembly
did adopt a resolution demanding that persons who attacked
or kidnapped diplomats or other officials of foreign
governments or international organizations be extradited or
prosecuted.[40]

Consultation and exchange of information and views
were also carried on by the State Department, primarily
through the mechanism of the working group. The principal
exchanges of intelligence were with Interpol (the International Criminal Police Organization) and the Organization of
American States, and with friendly governments also interested in curbing international terrorism.[41] In practice,
"friendly" governments were those to which the United States
was bound by treaty ties.

Where domestic terrorism posed the problem, the same
complexities existed. The FBI was the principal federal
agency responsible for combating terrorism, then as now. It
could call upon other federal agencies, including the
military forces, for help in crisis situations. However,
there is a fine line between certain terrorist acts and
common crimes which remain the responsibility of local law
enforcement agencies. While a terrorist act is in progress,
it may not be easy to determine whether the motive is
terrorism or ordinary criminal conduct, so that it may not
be clear whether the FBI should even be called in, much less
whether it should assume primary responsibility for taking
countermeasures.[42]

---

[40]Ibid., p. 3135.

[41]Ibid., p. 3136.

[42]Brian M. Jenkins, George Tanham, Eleanor
Weinstein, and Gerald Sullivan, U.S. Preparation for Future
Low-Level Conflict (Santa Monica, Calif.: Rand Corporation,
July 1977) p. 5.

During the 1974 congressional hearings on terrorism, one witness pointed out the confusion that could arise in determining responsibility for domestic terrorist incidents:

> . . . It certainly can get confusing. We have a State police captain, a local police chief, an FBI agent, then we have a postal inspector because the threat came through the mail--and it all started over here where the sheriff had the original jurisdiction. Believe me, all that can get complicated.
>
> Then we superimpose over that a board of experts; then in the end we have 20 people who want to run the thing.[43]

In the case where a federal crime such as kidnapping was involved, the FBI would normally head the team attempting to solve the problem. In other cases, the local chief of police would normally be in charge, with the support, if requested, of the FBI and other federal and state agencies. As indicated in the testimony, considerable confusion could result and there was no assurance that the best-qualified individual or organization would assume the command role.

Jurisdictional problems were less complex in cases of aircraft hijacking. The Federal Aviation Administration (FAA) of the Department of Transportation was the lead agency, chairing working groups and requesting help from other parts of the government as required. The aircraft hijacking problem was less complex because aircraft can only take off and land at facilities under the authority of the FAA. Moreover, aircraft hijackings were the first domestic and international terrorist acts to attract the attention of governments. The International Civil Aviation Organization adopted various resolutions on April 10, 1969, July 7, 1971, June 19, 1972, February 28, 1973, August 20, 1973, August 30, 1973, September 21, 1973, and March 22, 1974, dealing with general and specific problems involved in aircraft hijackings.[44] This record of action contrasts strikingly with the inability of the United Nations to adopt meaningful resolutions on the general subject of terrorism.

The Nixon administration also adopted a new policy in dealing with terrorist demands. Before 1972, the United States had no clear-cut policy, preferring to deal with each

---

[43]James Kelly, in *Terrorism, Part 1*, Hearings, p. 3074.

[44]Yonah Alexander, Marjorie Ann Browne, and Allan S. James, eds., *Control of Terrorism: International Documents* (New York: Crane Russak, 1979), pp. 165-83.

case on its own merits. C. Burke Elbrick, American ambassador to Brazil, was kidnapped on September 4, 1969, by
dissident elements who demanded the release of 14 political
prisoners in exchange for his safe return. The United
States pressed the Brazilian government to accede to these
terrorist demands, and the Brazilians reluctantly agreed.
Elbrick, a senior Foreign Service officer, was freed
unharmed.[45] A year later, Dan Mitrione, a comparatively
junior Foreign Service reserve officer, was kidnapped in
Uruguay for a similar reason. The State Department refused
to intervene, and Mitrione was eventually found dead.[46]
The implication was that an ambassador who had previously
been an assistant secretary of state for European affairs
was worth saving; a reserve officer who had come to the
Foreign Service via the ranks of the police did not merit
extraordinary efforts by his government to save his life.

After the attack on Israeli athletes at the 1972
Olympic Games in Munich, a clear-cut policy of no conces-
sions was adopted by the Cabinet Committee to Combat
Terrorism, and that policy was endorsed by the president.
An early test of the policy came in March, 1973, when eight
Palestinians of the Black September Faction seized the Saudi
Arabian embassy in Khartoum, Sudan, during a farewell party
for George Curtis Moore, the departing deputy chief of the
American embassy. The terrorists allowed most of the guests
to leave, keeping only Moore, Ambassador Cleo A. Noel, Jr.,
a Belgian diplomat, and two Arab diplomats. They demanded
the release of hundreds of political prisoners around the
world, including Sirhan Sirhan, Robert Kennedy's assassin.
The Nixon administration followed a curious course of
action. William Macomber, Jr., a senior State Department
official, was sent to Khartoum from Washington to negotiate
the hostages' release. Macomber was a political appointee
with great experience in congressional liaison but no
experience in the Middle East and very little in external
political matters. However, before he reached Khartoum,
President Nixon announced at a press conference that the
United States would not give in to blackmail. Shortly
thereafter, the terrorists surrendered to the Sudanese
authorities, but the Belgian and the two Americans were
found dead on the premises.[47]

---

[45]C. Burke Elbrick, in Terrorism, Part 2, Hearings,
pp. 3114-32.

[46]Robert A. Liston, Terrorism (Nashville, Tenn.:
Thomas Nelson, 1977), p. 118; U.S., Department of State, The
Biographic Register, 1968-1969 (Washington, D.C.: Department
of State, 1969), p. 494.

[47]New York Times, 1, 2, 3, and 4 March 1973, p. 1.

The United States continued to practice the no-concession policy throughout the remainder of the Nixon administration. In May, 1973, Terrance Leonhardy, a career Foreign Service officer serving as a consular official in Mexico, was kidnapped by leftist militants. They demanded the release of 30 political prisoners and the publication of their political demands. The State Department advised the Mexican government not to accede to these demands, but the Mexicans complied anyway and Leonhardy was released. In March, 1974, John Patterson, another career Foreign Service officer serving in a consular capacity in Mexico, was also kidnapped, and a large sum of money was demanded for his release. Although Patterson's family tried to raise the money, the United States government refused to cooperate and Patterson was killed.[48]

The Ford Administration

Considered next is the administration of President Gerald R. Ford (August, 1974--January, 1977). Ford's primary problem was to reestablish confidence in the government in a country wracked by the Watergate scandal and the near impeachment of a president.

In May, 1975, President Ford had the opportunity to react to a terrorist action by the newly formed Communist government of Cambodia. The U.S. merchant ship Mayaguez was seized by Cambodian forces on May 12, 1975, while off the island of Tang in the Gulf of Siam. The Mayaguez was a commercial vessel plying the usual shipping lanes in the region. When the Cambodians refused to permit the vessel to continue on its way, the United States assaulted Tang Island with an amphibious Marine landing while American planes attacked nearby airfields. The Cambodians released the vessel and its crew almost immediately after the attacks began. There was some criticism of the military action, based on the fact that 38 military lives were lost in the ground and air attacks in order to secure the release of a ship with a crew of 39.[49] On the other hand, the attack was in line with a tough no-concession policy and was designed to convince other nations that the United States would react vigorously to terrorist attacks on its vital interests.

A dismantling of the massive domestic intelligence mechanism developed during the Nixon administration also proceeded. Most of the White House personnel involved in domestic espionage were imprisoned, as was Attorney General John Mitchell. A blue-ribbon commission headed by Vice President Nelson Rockefeller reported on June 10, 1975, that

---

[48]Liston, p. 121.

[49]New York Times, 13, 14, and 15 May 1975, p. 1.

the CIA had engaged in massive domestic operations in violation of its basic charter but in response to the Nixon
administration's orders. Records had been maintained on
some 300,000 persons and groups in the United States, and
this effort had involved infiltration of agents into black,
antiwar, and political organizations, monitoring of overseas
phone calls, mail surveillance, and drug-testing. Information about assassination plots against foreign leaders was
developed but not made public. These and other illegal
activities were halted by the Ford administration, and
congressional oversight committees were established to make
certain that such abuses were not resumed in the future.[50]

The mechanisms developed by Nixon to combat terrorism were not changed during Ford's presidency. Neither was
there any alteration in the basic policy of refusal to
negotiate with terrorists or to accede to their demands.
This policy continued producing mixed results. On September
27, 1974, Barbara Hutchinson, the USIS (United States
Information Service) director in Santo Domingo, capital of
the Dominican Republic, was kidnapped, held for a ransom of
$1 million, and used in an attempt to have 36 political
prisoners released. When their demands were not met, the
terrorists settled for free passage out of the country,
releasing Hutchinson unharmed.[51]   On February 25, 1975,
however, the American consular agent in Cordoba, Argentina,
John Patrick Egan, was kidnapped by a group of armed men who
demanded the release of four of their Montoneros colleagues.
When the prisoners were not released within 48 hours as
demanded, Egan was executed.[52] The no-ransom policy was
circumvented in Beirut when United States Army Colonel
Ernest Morgan was kidnapped. The kidnappers demanded that
the American embassy distribute food and building supplies
in a poor Muslim neighborhood. The PLO, the Lebanese
government, and the Syrian government used their good
offices, and a group of wealthy Lebanese and Palestinians
organized and financed the distribution of food supplies in
a Beirut slum in order to gain the colonel's release.[53]   In
one case, therefore, the terrorists capitulated to the
no-ransom policy and settled for leaving the country. In
the second case, the policy resulted in the death of a
consular agent. In the third case, the policy was circumvented, as it was in many of the cases of the kidnapping of
private American citizens during the Ford administration.

---

[50]New York Times 11 June 1975, p. 1.

[51]U.S., Department of State, Significant Terrorist
Incidents, 1970-1980 (Washington, D.C.: Department of State,
n.d.), no page numbers, incidents are reported by date.

[52]Ibid.

[53]Ibid.

It is worth noting that, following President Ford's swift use of force to free the <u>Mayaguez</u> from the Cambodians in May, 1975, there were relatively few attacks on American official personnel and property during the balance of his term in office. The chief targets were American businessmen and American private property.

The Carter Administration

The Ford administration was followed by that of President Jimmy Carter (January, 1977--January, 1981). President Carter made a number of changes in the federal government's mechanisms and policies for dealing with terrorism.

Like his immediate predecessor, Carter issued orders to his CIA director establishing clear limits to agency intelligence operations directed against Americans both at home and abroad. At home, activity was restricted to the traditional debriefings of Americans returning home from "interesting" areas, and of CIA personnel. Abroad, only those Americans suspected of being foreign intelligence agents were to be targeted. Carter's instructions to Admiral Stansfield Turner were nearly identical in substance to those issued to George Bush by President Ford.[54]

Nevertheless, "the collection of intelligence about terrorism" was accorded "a high priority."[55] A great deal of useful intelligence was being acquired as a consequence of intergovernmental cooperation. In terms of American collection of intelligence about terrorism, major questions included these:

> . . . How much information should the U.S. Government collect about its own citizens? Where should we draw the line between defending ourselves against terrorist plots and becoming an instrument of "big brother"?[56]

Under Nixon, the line had been drawn in the direction of learning as much as possible about any conceivable threat; under Ford and Carter, the pendulum swung in the opposite direction.

---

[54]Stansfield Turner, "The CIA Shouldn't Spy on Americans," <u>Washington Post</u>, 1 November 1981, p. C-7.

[55]Anthony C. E. Quainton, "Terrorism: Do Something! But What?" <u>Department of State Bulletin</u> 79 (September 1979):62.

[56]Ibid.

In September, 1977, the Carter administration made a number of changes in the government's structures for dealing with terrorism. At the highest level of the new hierarchy, the structure of the National Security Council (NSC) was strengthened by establishing the Special Coordination Committee (SCC) to handle such matters as crisis management, jurisdictional disputes, issues requiring coordination in developing options, and the implementation of presidential decisions. The committee oversaw sensitive intelligence activities undertaken on presidential authority and arms control evaluation.[57]

The SCC was chaired by Zbigniew Brzezinski, assistant to the president for national security affairs. In addition to the statutory members of the NSC, other senior officials, including the secretary of the treasury, the attorney general, the United States representative to the United Nations, the director of the Office of Management and Budget, the chairman of the Council of Economic Advisers, the director of the Arms Control and Disarmament Agency, the chairman of the Joint Chiefs of Staff, and the secretary of energy, were asked to attend appropriate SCC meetings in person or through a deputy.[58]

Under the SCC was the Executive Committee on Terrorism (ECT), consisting of representatives of the departments of State, Defense, Justice, Treasury, Transportation, and Energy, and of the CIA and the NSC staff. The ECT was chaired by the representative of the Department of State, with the representative of the Department of Justice acting as deputy chairman. The ECT was responsible for handling matters of government-wide policy formulation and operational coordination. Its primary concerns were with the response to major terrorism incidents and related issues, including the periodic testing of response capabilities. It was also responsible for making certain that long-range antiterrorist program planning and analysis took place. Agencies normally assigned experienced officers of medium rank and appropriate experience to the ECT.[59]

The State Department's Working Group on Terrorism (WGT) continued in existence but with lower rank, expanded membership, and altered responsibilities. Chaired by the State Department representative (with the Department of Justice representative as deputy chairman), the WGT consisted of representatives of 29 agencies with a major or

---

[57]Anthony C. E. Quainton, "U.S. Antiterrorism Program," Department of State Bulletin 80 (July 1980):76.

[58]"Uncle Sam's Antiterrorism Plan," Security Management, February 1980, p. 41.

[59]Ibid.

minor interest in antiterrorism activities. In addition to
State and Justice, members included representatives of the
Agency for International Development, the Arms Control and
Disarmament Agency, the Central Intelligence Agency, the
Defense Intelligence Agency, the Department of the Army, the
Department of Commerce, the Department of Energy, the
Department of Transportation, the Department of the Trea-
sury, the Federal Aviation Administration, the Federal
Bureau of Investigation, the Federal Preparedness Agency,
the Immigration and Naturalization Service, the Center for
Disease Control, the Joint Chiefs of Staff, the Law Enforce-
ment Assistance Administration, the District of Columbia
Police Department, the National Security Agency, the Nuclear
Regulatory Commission, the Office of Management and Budget,
the Office of the Secretary of Defense, the U.S. Coast
Guard, the U.S. Customs Service, the United States mission
to the United Nations, the U.S. Postal Service, the Secret
Service, and the U.S. Marshal Service.[60]

Because of the large number of agencies involved in
the WGT and their differing interests and areas of expertise, the full group met periodically but worked primarily
through a number of specialized committees. A higher-level
committee dealt with incident management (the Committee on
Contingency Planning and Crisis Management). Other committees dealt with such matters as assessing physical security
at U.S. government installations at home and abroad,
evaluating and proposing new international initiatives,
establishing research priorities, and developing guidelines
for a coordinated public affairs posture by federal agencies
during a terrorist attack.[61]

The incident management committee of the WGT, under
the direct supervision of its senior staff, concentrated its
attention on interagency policy issues and the federal
government's crisis management capabilities. The committee
reviewed extensively the government's antiterrorism training
capabilities and the policy issues involved in such
training. The committee also reviewed the federal government's handling of each specific terrorist incident.
Attempts were also made to clarify lines of authority and
jurisdiction, including a formal memorandum of understanding
between the State Department and the Federal Aviation
Administration dealing with responsibilities in international hijacking incidents.[62]

---

[60]Ibid., p. 43.

[61]Anthony C. E. Quainton, "Testimony," in Omnibus
Antiterrorism Act of 1979, Hearings Before the Committee on
Governmental Affairs, Senate, 96th Congress, 1st Sess.
(Washington, D.C.: Government Printing Office, 1979), p. 11.

[62]Ibid.

The lead agency concept became firmly established during the Carter administration. Under the Constitution and laws of the United States, state and local governments are primarily responsible for the protection of life and property and for maintaining public order. Terrorist acts are also crimes under state and some federal statutes. Most major acts of terrorism are violations of both state and federal laws, so that concurrent criminal jurisdiction is the rule. Depending on the nature of the terrorist act and the capabilities of local law enforcement officials, federal officials can either act or defer to the local authorities. Whichever one acts, the other is expected to provide assistance.[63]

The Department of State is the lead agency for response to international terrorist attacks occurring outside the United States. It has a major interest in any terrorist action involving foreign diplomatic or other official personnel.

Terrorist incidents inside the United States are normally managed by the Department of Justice. One exception is provided by USC 1356 (c), which states that the administrator of the Federal Aviation Administration shall have exclusive responsibility for the direction of any law enforcement activity affecting the safety of persons aboard aircraft in flight. When the doors of the aircraft are closed, the FAA has primary responsibility; when they are open with the plane on the ground, Justice is normally the lead agency. Within the Department of Justice, the lead agency for the management of most terrorist incidents is the FBI.[64]

As terrorism policy evolved under President Carter, the attorney general delegated his authority to the deputy attorney general in all cases involving terrorism in the United States. Should an incident occur, this official would supervise the operations of the task force established for the emergency. The tactical response to the incident would be handled by the FBI special-agent-in-charge at the scene, under the supervision of the director in Washington. The deputy attorney general would ensure coordination of the total federal response. The FBI has contingency plans for a variety of possible incidents, specialists in hostage negotiations, a special operations and research unit

---

[63]"Uncle Sam's Antiterrorism Plan," p. 43.

[64]Quainton, in Omnibus Antiterrorism Act of 1979, Hearings, p. 11.

concentrating exclusively on terrorism and hostage situations, SWAT units, and a terrorism research and bomb data unit.[65]

An example of the function of these structures came on August 17, 1978, when two Croatian gunmen seized control of the West German consulate in Chicago, taking eight hostages. They demanded that the West German government release a Croatian held in Cologne and provide assurances that it would not permit his extradition to Yugoslavia. After ten hours of negotiation, the two men released their hostages and surrendered to police. Both the FBI and the State Department were involved in the resolution of the incident, as were the Chicago police.[66] According to Ambassador Quainton, "the inter-relationships that we have created have ensured that, in crises, the various responsible parts of the Federal, State, and local governments work effectively together."[67]

Among the international initiatives taken by the Carter administration, one of the more important was the decision made at the Bonn (West Germany) Summit in July, 1978, concerning hijacking. Essentially, the eight participating governments agreed to "cease immediately their commercial air service to, and to initiate action to halt incoming flights from, countries which refuse to prosecute or extradite aircraft hijackers or return hijacked aircraft."[68]

Through the State Department, the Carter administration also tried to obtain ratification and accessions to the UN Convention on the Prevention and Punishment of Crimes Against Internationally Protected Persons, Including Diplomatic Agents, and to the Tokyo, Hague, and Montreal conventions against air piracy and sabotage. Only some 40 countries were parties to the UN convention, whereas more than 100 had adhered to one or more of the air piracy and sabotage conventions in 1979.[69]

---

[65]"Uncle Sam's Antiterrorism Plan," p. 45.

[66]Brian M. Jenkins, Embassies Under Siege (Santa Monica, Calif.: Rand Corporation, January 1981), p. 33.

[67]Quainton, in Omnibus Antiterrorism Act of 1979, Hearings, p. 12.

[68]U.S., "Department Statement," July 28, 1978, Department of State Bulletin 78 (September 1978):5.

[69]Quainton, "Terrorism: Do Something! But What?" p. 63.

The basic policy on yielding to terrorist demands remained formally unchanged during the Carter years. As stated by Secretary of State Vance, "We have made clear to all that we will reject terrorist blackmail. We have clearly and repeatedly stated our intention to reject demands for ransom or for the release of prisoners."[70]

The great terrorist trauma of the Carter administration was the takeover of the American embassy in Teheran by a large group of Iranian militants on November 4, 1979. A number of procedures and policies appear to have been ignored or altered in this particular instance. Although the State Department had spent millions of dollars on strengthening potential targets at its overseas posts, the embassy was induced to capitulate after a siege of approximately two hours.[71] The two hours were not used effectively by embassy personnel, to destroy sensitive files and equipment, even though every embassy and consular post is required to have destruction plans and equipment. There was a series of major intelligence failures, starting with estimates of Iranian reaction to the Shah's entry into the United States and ending with the inability to understand the nature of the political process in revolutionary Iran. The crisis was handled at the working level by a task force headed by the assistant secretary of state for Near Eastern affairs. The president was intimately involved in all major policy decisions, assisted by the secretary of state, the undersecretary, and the national security adviser, along with other cabinet officers and the director of the CIA. An informal military committee was formed by Brzezinski, including the secretary of defense, the chairman of the Joint Chiefs of Staff, and the director of the CIA. This "committee met two or three times a week to consider military options and devised the rescue attempt which was eventually approved by the President."[72] During this period, the elaborate machinery set in place by President Carter to handle problems of terrorism was virtually ignored.

Ultimately, the United States was able to secure the release of the hostages without violating the letter of the no-ransom policy. Under the terms of the agreement finally

---

[70]Cyrus R. Vance, "Terrorism: Scope of the Threat and Need for Effective Legislation," Department of State Bulletin 78 (March 1978):54.

[71]One hundred million dollars had been spent by 1979 on physical security overseas, according to Quainton, "Terrorism: Do Something! But What?" p. 62.

[72]Terence Smith, "Putting the Hostages' Lives First," New York Times Magazine, Special Edition, 1981, p. 78.

worked out, Iran received assets that the United States had frozen early in the crisis but not a penny more; the United States received its kidnapped personnel. On the other hand, some observers believed that negotiating at all with a regime that had countenanced or encouraged such an unprecedented breach of civilized conduct was a betrayal of the national honor.[73] Experts in the State Department advised Vance that the United States should "do and say nothing about the hostages publicly, but advise Iranians in private that we are going to tighten the screws on them, politically and economically, and come down hard if they do anything to harm the hostages."[74] This advice was never relayed to President Carter.[75]

The aura of impotence which surrounded the Carter administration in this particular attempt to deal with a terrorist act may have done much to cause his defeat in the 1980 presidential election. "If President Carter had gotten the hostages out, he might well have won re-election."[76] For months, the administration negotiated with Iranian public officials who had no power to make a deal, botching the military attempt to free the hostages.

The Reagan Administration

During his election campaign, President Reagan spoke repeatedly of the need for the United States to take the lead. Although he did not mention Iran by name, his meaning was clear when, in his October 19, 1980, televised speech, he said: "In sharing the outrage against terrorism, I will direct the resources of my administration against this scourge of civilization and toward expansion of our cooperation with other nations combating terrorism in its many forms."[77] During the campaign, he called the Iranians "barbarians" and "common criminals" while suggesting that

---

[73]Former Secretary of State Henry Kissinger stated in a Houston, Texas, speech that the United States should end its policy of "self-abasement" in dealing with the Iranian regime. Cited in ibid., p. 83.

[74]Ibid., p. 101.

[75]Ibid.

[76]Steven R. Weisman, "For America, A Painful Reawakening," New York Times Magazine, Special Edition, 1981, p. 114. in the fight against international terrorism.

[77]Rowland Evans and Robert Novak, The Reagan Revolution (New York: E. P. Dutton, 1981), p. 195.

they would find it far more difficult to negotiate with him than with President Carter.[78]

Newly elected President Reagan chose the occasion of the formal welcome of the freed hostages to the White House to proclaim a more assertive American stance against international terrorism, using the Iranian militants as examples.[79]

> . . . Let terrorists be aware that when the rules of international behavior are violated, our policy will be one of swift and effective retribution. We hear it said that we live in an era of limits to our powers. Well, let it also be understood that there are limits to our patience.[80]

The Reagan administration has blamed the Soviet Union for aiding and abetting, if not actually orchestrating, terrorism around the world. In a speech on January 29, 1981, then Secretary of State Haig accused the Soviet Union of promoting international terrorism.[81] The following day, the acting State Department spokesman said that Soviet actions in the terrorist field included Soviet financial support, training and arming of PLO guerrillas, the use of Cuban and Libyan surrogates as conduits to terrorist groups, the support of guerrillas in El Salvador and South-West Africa (Namibia), and broadcasting approval of the holding of American hostages.[82] On the same day, President Reagan, while not using the word "terrorism," declared that the Soviet leadership reserved to itself the right "to commit any crime, to lie, to cheat."[83] Stern action against terrorism was thus elevated to a cardinal principle of American foreign policy, and the Soviet Union was described as the prime instigator of terrorism throughout the world.

One of the signs of the tougher new policy was the shooting down of two Soviet-built Libyan SU-22 fighter

---

[78]Weisman, p. 120.

[79]Hedrick Smith, "An Assertive America," New York Times, 25 January 1981, p. 17.

[80]New York Times, 30 January 1981, p. 4.

[81]Ibid.

[82]Ibid.

[83]Ibid.

planes in international airspace over international waters in the Mediterranean. The incident occurred on August 19, 1981, while the United States engaged in naval and air maneuvers in the Gulf of Sidra, claimed by Libya as within its territorial waters--a claim not accepted by most nations. On the following day, President Reagan defended the action of the American planes and stated that the United States would continue its policy of prompt retaliatory action to make its power "impressive to the enemies of freedom."[84] Although the maneuvers were not intended to provoke an incident, the president declared, "We decided it was time to recognize what are the international waters and to behave accordingly."[85] Under President Carter, American planes were prohibited from flying over the Gulf of Sidra. In recent months, Libya's leader, Colonel Muammar Qaddafi, has emerged as one of the principal sponsors of international terrorism, which explains the desire of the Reagan administration to challenge him.

There are indications that the Reagan approach will be oriented toward law and order rather than civil liberties. Attorney General William French Smith declared on October 28, 1981, that he would like to see Congress rewrite the criminal sentencing rules to shift the emphasis away from rehabilitation and toward "punishment, deterrence, and protection of the public."[86] He also called for tougher bail provisions, mandatory prison terms for certain crimes, and a federal death penalty in limited circumstances.

Under the terms of Executive Order 12333 of December 4, 1981, the CIA is enabled once again to engage in domestic intelligence activities in coordination with the FBI. Intelligence activities are defined circularly in the executive order as "all activities that agencies within the intelligence community are authorized to conduct pursuant to this order."

Few changes have been made in the response mechanisms developed by previous administrations. The National Security Council and its antiterrorist appendage have been downgraded in importance. Because President Reagan prefers to employ cabinet government, the State Department's Office

---

[84]"The Month in Review," Current History 80 (October 1981):349.

[85]Ibid.

[86]Mary Thornton, "Attorney General Emphasizes Punishment and Deterrence," Washington Post, 29 October 1981, p. A-10.

for Combating Terrorism appears to be playing a greater role than it did under President Carter.

The work of the office is based on five principles: improved intelligence, better physical security, crisis management, preparedness, and international cooperation. Improved intelligence is to be achieved by a major intelligence effort and through closer intelligence ties with friendly countries. Physical security involves the concept of building "safehavens" within diplomatic and consular posts where personnel will be safe for a time until the host government can act or until destruction procedures are carried out. There has been no change in crisis management and preparedness procedures, nor in the effort to develop effective international action against terrorism.[87]

The organizational structure of the Reagan anti-terrorism campaign does not appear entirely to have coalesced more than two years after the president assumed office. It was reported that a task force of the State Department, Defense Department, and CIA had been established to study policy alternatives on the best way to cope with Cuban military support for militant groups in Latin America. The NSC was completely bypassed as a result of the influence of then Deputy Secretary of State William P. Clark, who has his personal channels to the White House.[88] The confusion that developed when the president was shot and the secretary of state claimed that he, rather than the vice president, was in charge of government is another case in point.

Domestically, the Reagan administration has had noteworthy success against terrorism, although luck rather than the merits of the response structure may be responsible. The robbery of a Brink's truck in which two policemen and one Brink's guard died resulted in the arrest of a key Weather Underground leader (Katherine Boudin) who had been sought for some ten years. Working back from this captured leader, the police have uncovered a complex network of associated radicals, safehouses, and arms caches. Implicated in the robbery and associated with the Weather Underground are the Black Liberation Army, the Republic of New Africa, and various Puerto Rican liberation groups. The capture of Boudin "has given lawmen the tools and the

[87]"U.S. Terrorism Policy Defined," Defense and Foreign Affairs Daily, Main Edition, part II, 8 April 1981, pp. 1-2.

[88]Don Oberdorfer and Martin Schram, "Haig Believes a Reagan Aide is Campaigning Against Him," Washington Post, 4 November 1981, pp. A-1, A-9; Hedrick Smith, "Feuding Over Foreign Policy Roles is Renewed Within Administration," New York Times, 24 March 1981, pp. 1, 6.

opportunity to finally break the remnants of the radicals' operations that has eluded them for so many years, at least in the eyes of some officials."[89]

Internationally, the Reagan activism in military policy has sparked protests in a number of European nations. There has been a revival of terrorism in West Germany--after two years of relative quiet. In March, 1981, a building in Giessen believed to belong to American intelligence services was bombed, as was a military building in Frankfurt. The West German Red Army Faction, which had been inactive for some two years, claimed credit for these actions. In April, a nine-pound bomb was discovered and defused at a military community center on the U.S. Air Force base in Wiesbaden. On August 31, a powerful bomb exploded outside the headquarters of United States and NATO Air Force operations at Ramstein. Whereas the earlier incidents had resulted in loss of property only, the August blast injured 20 persons, including two senior officers, and also caused extensive property damage.[90]

Perceived Inadequacies of the
Federal Response Structure

One school of thought holds that the federal response structure is unnecessary, either because the terrorist threat has been overstated or because what is lacking is an understanding of the basic problem. In a long discussion of the Soviet link to international terrorism, Horner points out that the facts are readily available to any enterprising journalist. The PLO, for example, has publicly stated that it receives funds, equipment, and training from the Soviet Union, and the Soviet Union has never denied the link. The meaning of this "fact," however, depends on the views of the analyst examining the Palestinian problem. According to Horner, "overall, what has been missing in our confrontation with the phenomenon of Soviet-sponsored terrorism is not fact, but comprehension."[91] The federal response structure is geared to produce facts rather than ideas leading to comprehension.

The comprehension which would seem to be required includes an appreciation of the motives of those who engage

---

[89]Kathy Sawyer, "Police Push to Flush Out the Underground," Washington Post, 25 October 1981, p. A-2.

[90]Bradley Graham, "20 Injured by Bomb at U.S. Base," Washington Post, 1 September 1981, p. A-13.

[91]Charles Horner, "The Facts About Terrorism," Commentary 69 (June 1980):45.

in terrorist acts. When an Armenian terrorist strikes down
a Turkish official, that terrorist would seem to be expressing a hatred that has its roots in persecutions which took
place before World War I. However, there are comparatively
few religious or ethnic groups that cannot look back to
comparable treatment at some point in their history.
Moreover, the overwhelming majority of Armenians does not
undertake violent actions against Turkish nationals, much as
it might like to in its heart. Virtually nothing is written
about the motives of the Armenian terrorist in government
publications or in the scholarly or popular presses. What
is an American to think about a Croatian nationalist group
which hijacks an airplane to publicize a country that
existed only in the Middle Ages and which has very little
chance to ever come into existence again? Do the Basque
nationalists want independence from Spain, or do they
actually wish a Marxist Spain? The same question is
relevant in the case of the Provisional Wing of the IRA.

Lumping together all terrorist acts, as the federal
response structure tends to do while spending little time on
motives, can result in profound misunderstandings. Some
terrorist acts are political in the sense that they are
directed toward the achievement of a realizable political
goal. It is conceivable, for example, that the Palestinians
and the South African Bantus will, someday, realize their
political dreams. Other terrorists are merely acting on
some ancient hatred or utopian dream. They may have a right
to their hatred or their dream, but not a right to use
violence. Unless the federal response structure learns how
to distinguish between political and pathological terrorism,
it will be difficult for the United States government to act
with political wisdom.

The comprehension required also extends to distinctions between the tactics used by various terrorist groups.
The chronologies of terrorist acts published by the American
government and by the Rand Corporation do not discriminate
between major and minor, heinous and relatively innocuous,
acts. All are given equal weight in the sense that government spokesmen point with alarm to an increase of x percen-
tage points in the incidence of terrorism around the world
or in the United States. Some terrorist acts merely rattle
windows; others result in the loss of innocent lives. If,
in some particular year, there are many incidents of the
first kind and comparatively few of the second kind, is it
really accurate to state that the incidence of terrorism
increased during that year?

Also missing in the government and the Rand Corporation analyses is an idea regarding why the various terrorist
groups around the world accept Soviet assistance. The
attitude of the United States toward these groups would seem
to require some understanding on that score. Does accep-

tance of aid necessarily imply adherence to the Soviet world view? Alternatively, are such groups equally willing to accept aid from any source, including the United States?

These and related questions are not easy to answer. The degree of difficulty they involve may explain why so little attention has been paid to them. However, if a nation invests in a response structure, it has the right to expect more comprehension than that provided by statistical analyses. Most of the government output and much of the Rand material is statistical in nature. The implications of the statistics are rarely explored to any great depth.

Selzer, by contrast, believes that terrorism is a phenomenon that has been greatly overpublicized:

> . . . Despite the availability of modern weapons and of sanctuaries in which to hide--and also despite the vulnerability of our densely packed cities--terrorists have proven to be remarkably impotent. A sober examination establishes that terrorists have caused very little destruction of either life or property, and that the political consequences of their assaults are negligible. No regime has fallen to terrorist attack, and no significant social, political, or economic changes have been brought about as a result of terrorist pressure.[92]

While the statement could be challenged in some of its details, it does seem true that terrorism counts far fewer victims than does common crime. "During the four years 1971 to 1975, one of America's most notorious terrorist groups, the Weather Underground, averaged one sixth of an attack per person per year!"[93] The implication is that terrorism could be handled as merely another aspect of common crime, using the existing federal, state, and local police forces in lieu of a large, specialized bureaucracy.

Shulman has found that current dogma regarding the Soviet Union is made up of the following four propositions: (1) the Soviet Union is the cause of all or most American problems in the world, including the problem of terrorism; (2) the balance of world power has shifted in favor of the Russians; (3) the Soviets are moving into a posture of greater aggressiveness in the world, and they are inherently

---

[92]Michael Selzer, Terrorist Chic: An Exploration of Violence in the Seventies (New York: Hawthorn Books, 1979), pp. 177-78.

[93]Ibid., p. 183.

and unchangeably aggressive; and (4) Soviet aggressiveness requires a more militant response, leading logically to a policy of active confrontation. He suggests that:

> The truth behind this dogma is not the reverse of these propositions, but rather that each of them requires a more differentiated analysis. The truth is far more complex than these oversimplifications. To act on these dogmas leads to self-defeating policies.[94]

The current dogma focuses on Soviet successes and overlooks the very real problems of the Soviets on the contemporary world scene--problems that include a hostile China, the need to wage low-level warfare in Afghanistan, the obvious defection from Communist ideals of many peoples behind the Iron Curtain, including those of Poland, and a series of economic fiascos, particularly in the agricultural realm. In the case of the first proposition, since it is almost certainly true that the Soviet Union supports terrorist groups, those who oppose the current dogma would be wrong to claim that it does not. The fact is that both of the superpowers have been accused of supporting terrorism when it suited their respective national interests. The bureaucratization of the study of terrorism, now largely the province of the government or of such large organizations as the Rand Corporation, is not likely to lead to differentiated analysis but to a kind of sterile orthodoxy.

In 1981, the National Republican Senatorial Committee issued a Special Report declaring that terrorism threatened United States national security.[95] The report pointed out that 642 persons were killed and 1,078 wounded in international terrorist attacks in 1980. During the same period, there were 278 separate attacks overseas. Since there is no "law at the moment that says you cannot go overseas and receive training in terrorist matters," the most that could legally be done would be to discuss the matter informally with the individual if he consented to do so. Not even a limited investigation could be undertaken.[96]

---

[94]Shulman, p. 19. Marshall Shulman is director of the Russian Institute at Columbia University and was special adviser to the secretary of state for Soviet affairs in the Carter administration.

[95]National Republican Senatorial Committee, "Terrorism Threatens U.S. National Security," Special Report, Washington, D.C., May 1981, p. 1.

[96]Ibid., pp. 24-25.

Intelligence and Counterintelligence

The State Department representative stated to the Subcommittee on Civil and Constitutional Rights in 1978 that "the Intelligence Community's activities in support of U.S. Government efforts to cope with terrorism have been effective and have contributed to our overall program."[97] According to Ambassador Quainton, all three facets of foreign intelligence--collection of information, analysis, and maintenance of an adequate data base--were working effectively.

Whether or not intelligence is, in fact, adequate is not a subject with which the literature in the field has concerned itself directly. The most important intelligence is classified and not available to the general public or even to most members of Congress. It seems obvious that the United States has been caught short by a number of important international developments; whether the fault lies in the intelligence or in a failure to heed intelligence warnings is not entirely clear. In the case of the negotiations with Iran over the hostages, it is clear that either the intelligence was not sound or it was ignored. Moreover, a Rand Corporation specialist on terrorism indicated that Rand reports are never discussed formally by the government client to which they are delivered. He continued:

> I think there could be more systematic exploitation of the knowledge and research done by the Rand Corporation and that done by other research institutions, that already exists. There is a considerable amount of knowledge in this area. I'm not persuaded that it is being systematically pursued.[98]

There is always a risk when a subject becomes "fashionable" that so much information about it becomes available that much of it is not used.

Apart from the quality of the product, which cannot be analyzed fairly in this study, the principal issue regarding intelligence involves the methods of collecting it. Under the Carter administration, terrorism was handled in accordance with the criminal statutes, and strict limits

---

[97]Anthony Quainton, in ibid., p. 55.

[98]Brian M. Jenkins, "Testimony," in An Act to Combat International Terrorism, Hearings Before the Committee on Governmental Affairs, Senate, 95th Congress, 2nd Sess. (Washington, D.C.: Government Printing Office, 1978), p. 112.

were placed on the activities of domestic and externally-oriented intelligence agencies. These safeguards will be removed by the Reagan administration in the interests of more effectively collecting intelligence. The CIA will be permitted to target some intelligence and conduct operations against domestic individuals and groups as directed by the president. The director of the American Civil Liberties Union has stated: "If broadly defined and pursued, terrorism investigations can overwhelm freedom of speech, association, and assembly . . . the worst elements of McCarthyism can be assembled."[99] On the other hand, Senator Jeremiah Denton of Alabama believes that intensified intelligence efforts are justified because if "we continue to ignore the threat, the sand in which we bury our heads will eventually bury our nation."[100]

The problems facing the United States are different from those which divided the nation during the Nixon administration. The intelligence guidelines apparently favored by the Reagan administration are similar to those implemented by Nixon, but the intent appears to be different. The Nixon team was faced with a large, angry, and frequently lawless opposition to the Vietnam War. The Reagan team appears to believe that almost all terrorists are working directly or indirectly for the Soviet Union; the target of wiretapping, mail covers, informants, and surreptitious entries would presumably be much smaller than during the Nixon era. Even so, the proposed new guidelines will be politically divisive.[101]

The Policy of No Concessions

The traditional U.S. policy has been to "make no concessions to terrorist blackmail."[102] Whether or not this policy was carried out during the Iranian hostage crisis has been debated. Occasionally, the policy has been circumvented as indicated earlier. Criticism of the policy has come from those who believe that it unnecessarily jeopardizes American lives and from those who believe that it has not been tough enough.

---

[99]James Neff, "Internal Security: Right Sees Threat, Left Charges McCarthyism," San Francisco Examiner & Chronicle, 13 September 1981, p. A-16.

[100]Ibid.

[101]Victor Navasky, "Security and Terrorism," Nation 232 (14 February 1981):176-86.

[102]U.S., Department of State, "U.S. Policy on Terrorism: Air Force Policy Letter for Commanders," Department of State Bulletin 79 (May 1979):31.

C. Burke Elbrick, American ambassador to Brazil and a veteran at the time of 38 years in the Foreign Service, was kidnapped by six Brazilian left-wing terrorists on September 4, 1969. The terrorists demanded the release of 16 political prisoners in Brazilian jails. Thjails. The Brazilian government complied and Elbrick was released four days after being seized. Elbrick expressed his opposition to the no-concession policy in the following terms:

> Mr. Chairman, I for one think it is a pretty lousy policy. There is sort of a built-in inconsistency in this type of policy. For one thing, American businessmen are kidnapped, for example, in Argentina, and the U.S. Government does not say to these companies, "You can't pay ransom." They wouldn't think of doing that. But they say to other governments, "You should not pay ransom for the return of American diplomats."
>
> In the Sudan last year at Khartoum, our Ambassador and the Minister were kidnapped and held in the Saudi Arabian Embassy. While the State Department negotiator was en route to Khartoum, the President made a statement to the effect that we should never be blackmailed by terrorists. . . . Following that statement and before a negotiator could arrive in Khartoum, the kidnappers machinegunned these two men. Then in Haiti . . . Clinton E. Knox who was our Ambassador there, was kidnapped. . . . The kidnappers had demanded the release of some political prisoners and a sum of money. When the young President of Haiti heard about our policy, he said, "But Mr. Knox is our friend and we must negotiate," and so they did.
>
> I don't know if this policy of the U.S. Government is going to have the effect of destroying our image or anything, but it makes for certain misunderstandings abroad, in any case.[103]

To emphasize his contention that a double standard was involved, Elbrick asked the House Committee on Internal Security to consider whether or not there would be negotiations if a member of the cabinet or a member of the president's family were kidnapped instead of a diplomat. Because a diplomat is of lower rank does not make the existing policy "a humanitarian way of looking at things."[104]

---

[103]C. Burke Elbrick, in An Act to Combat International Terrorism, Hearings, p. 3122.

[104]Ibid., p. 3123.

Elbrick agreed that the reasoning behind the policy was that the risks of kidnapping would be increased if the American government were to alter its policy. However, "it is a rather tempting thought that such a policy would eventually do away with kidnapping as a political instrument. But meanwhile you will probably lose several more ambassadors."[105] As for improving security for diplomats, Elbrick was afraid that any practical measures that could be taken would ruin the ambassador's peaceful mission by making it difficult for him to travel widely and meet a great many people.[106]

Ambassador Hoffacker, special assistant to the secretary of state and coordinator for combating terrorism, defended the policy, while admitting that there was constant debate within the Foreign Service regarding its wisdom. He concluded that, on balance, "we were wise to have instituted this policy. Morale is an important factor in this, but there is another factor as well—saving lives."[107]

Allan Luks, a New York attorney with experience in dealing with terrorists in Venezuela, told the House Committee that the hard-line policy on no negotiation with terrorists ought to be modified. In most cases,

> . . . if a revolutionary can seize a group of hostages and get whatever his demands are for his cause . . . it will continue to promote those groups. There, the no-ransom posture makes sense.

> . . . However, there comes a time in human life when no strict policy makes sense. As we all saw in the Middle East recently where basically you had terrorists [who] were there to spread terror in the community in order to bring down society. The only way they could be satisfied would be to have this fear recognized. Yet I would hope to God, if it ever came down to that kind of situation in the United States, we would give in.[108]

Luks was arguing for a posture of greater flexibility than that adopted by successive American administrations.

---

[105]Ibid.

[106]Ibid., p. 3153.

[107]Lewis Hoffacker, in _Terrorism, Part 2_, Hearings, p. 3153.

[108]Allan Luks, in ibid., p. 3200.

Robert L. Rabe, deputy chief of policy of the Washington, D.C. Metropolitan Police Department and head of the Special Operations Division, generally agreed with Luks' position. In any hostage situation, the primary concern of the authorities is to get the hostages out safely. Once the hostages have been freed or released, the next step is to apprehend the perpetrators of the act. Any policy that makes it impossible to bargain for the hostages' safety would, therefore, appear unsound.[109]

Dr. F. Gentry Harris, chief of psychiatry at the U.S. Public Health Service in San Francisco and a specialist in skyjacking psychology, also indicated that a flexible policy ought to be followed in acceding to terrorists' demands. The negotiating party should not agree to the terrorists' initial demands, but should attempt to scale them down before acceding to a lower level of demands. Asked by one of the members of the committee to comment on the State Department's policy of never paying ransom, Dr. Harris responded: "I am not so sure it should be as rigid and binding as it is."[110]

Frederick J. Hacker, a distinguished teaching psychiatrist, also addressed himself to the general policy of the United States in dealing with terrorist demands. Answering terrorism with terror was not a sound policy, he thought. History was replete with examples where terrorism used against opponents resulted in the creation of a totalitarian regime (the Soviet Union, Nazi Germany).

. . . Internationally, the policy of the United States [was] not to pay ransom but to permit foreign governments and foreign as well as American companies to pay ransom. . . . This makes for the type of confusion that renders it totally impossible to develop any kind of policy.[111]

The same confusion existed in the domestic Patty Hearst case, where the family was encouraged to carry out negotiations while the official stand of the FBI was to condone it but not to favor it. Hacker pointed out that terrorists often wish to have a society they despise execute them; thus a policy of force may merely be playing into their hands.

Speaking for the International Association of Chiefs of Police, James Kelly also expressed doubts about the government's no-ransom policy. Domestically, he doubted

---

[109]Robert L. Rabe, in ibid., p. 3222.

[110]F. Gentry Harris, in Terrorism, Part 1, Hearings, p. 2073.

[111]Frederick J. Hacker, in ibid., p. 3015.

that the policy would work because no jury would convict a
father for paying ransom for his daughter's release, even if
Congress were to pass a law prohibiting it. Moreover,
people would be extremely reluctant to report kidnappings to
the police or the FBI. In terms of international situations, he observed:

> I have been in military service and if I had
> been killed . . . certainly my family and others
> would have known I was placing myself in that
> jeopardy. I would also hope that the State
> Department is taking all the precautions they can
> to protect the individuals. That individual is in
> a kind of a cold war situation, but war it is.
> Cold is simply an adjective. When you talk about
> the industrial people--if they were to have a
> no-ransom policy, those people would simply walk
> off the job.[112]

The statement appears to equate State Department overseas
personnel with members of the military, except that Foreign
Service officers do not ordinarily go into the field with
guns, ammunition, steel helmets, and other equipment. The
comparison is therefore somewhat questionable, but it makes
important distinctions and assumptions which will be considered in chapter 4 of this study.

An agronomist kidnapped by the Tupamaros in
Uruguay--and held by them for seven months under very difficult conditions before being released after a heart
attack--also commented on the no-ransom policy. Dr. Claude
L. Fly pointed out that if the government of a nation adopts
a no-negotiations policy, it is very difficult for the
United States to interfere when one of its nationals is
kidnapped. This was the case in Uruguay, where President
Pacheco took the attitude that the Tupamaros were criminals
with whom no one should negotiate except with guns. "That
is the reason Dan Mitrione was shot. That is the reason
Gomide and I were held so long. When the Tupamaros tried
later to exchange me for the publication of their manifesto,
Pacheco threatened to take over the media if they did
publish this material."[113] Fly thought the no-ransom policy
was wrong. Of 42 individuals kidnapped abroad up to August
1, 1973, 33 had no protection at all at the time they were
kidnapped and the others had at the most one or two guards.
Thirty-two kidnappings involved demands; 17 demands were met
and the kidnap victim was promptly released. Where the
demands were not met, 67 percent of the victims were killed,

---

[112]James Kelly, in ibid., p. 3073.

[113]Claude L. Fly, in Terrorism, Part 3, Hearings,
p. 3975.

13 percent were wounded, and 20 percent were released under special or accidental conditions.[114] As far as providing extraordinary protection for diplomats and consultants working abroad, he thought that such protection would affect adversely their ability to carry out their duties.

All of the officials currently in office who testified before the various committees of Congress looking into terrorism justified the no-ransom policy.

One private observer indicated that the government's policy of no ransom is not entirely what it seems to be.

The attitude of the Americans, who are be-deviled by hostage situations, is officially one of no negotiation with terrorists, but with modifying variations that allow discussions, and even intercession by private individuals. Their method is very flexible and experimental.[115]

For Kupperman and Trent, the fundamental policy choice really depends on the number of individuals involved:

On the face of it, government policy should prohibit concessions to terrorists. This posture may indeed be appropriate when the lives of a handful of individuals are threatened. However, the policy of no substantive bargaining with terrorists would be reevaluated in the event that society was threatened with mass destruction of lives and property.[116]

The authors do not mention that the importance of the victim--a very high government official, for example--might also alter the desirability of a no-ransom policy.

Mickolus summarized the arguments for both the no-ransom policy and a flexible policy in considerable detail. He concluded that:

---

[114]Ibid., p. 3973.

[115]Edgar O'Ballance, Language of Violence: The Blood Politics of Terrorism (San Rafael, Calif.: Presidio Press, 1979), p. 333.

[116]Robert Kupperman and Darrell Trent, eds., Terrorism: Threat, Reality, Response (Stanford, Calif.: Hoover Institution Press of Stanford University, 1979), pp. 111-12.

The answer may be somewhere between a stated "no-ransom" position and a pragmatic view of on-thescene bargaining. It may be that we should aim at creating a new self-image for the terrorists by gaining their commitment to what can be presented as humanitarian policies, such as releasing some of their prisoners or allowing food and medical aid to be supplied. If the terrorists would agree to making incremental moves in this direction, we might be able to keep up the process of commitment and eventually make possible the release of all hostages. Such tactics appear to have been successful when applied and may represent an optimal mix of the advantages claimed by the two positions . . . discussed.[117]

One of the arguments against a no-ransom policy is that if it were universally applied and terrorists could no longer take hostages, they might turn to alternative, and probably more destructive, tactics.

The Response Mechanism

The inadequacies of the existing response mechanism can be pointed out in two different ways. The observer may state specifically what his objection is to the current system, or he may criticize it indirectly by suggesting improvements. Most of the inadequacies in the federal and local response mechanisms are in the second category and are considered next.

One of the nation's leading experts on terrorism and measures to combat it is Brian Jenkins of the Rand Corporation. In 1978, he testified before the Senate Committee on Governmental Affairs that the major gap in the response mechanism was an organization to bring experts in various fields together in a meaningful way.

---

[117]Edward F. Mickolus, "Negotiating for Hostages: A Policy Dilemma," in Contemporary Terrorism: Selected Readings, ed. John D. Elliott and Leslie K. Gibson (Gaithersburg, Md.: International Association of Chiefs of Police, 1978), p. 220.

There are efforts going on through the Department of Justice and the Federal Bureau of Investigation. . . . There are related but separate
efforts going on in [the] Department of State and
also within the Intelligence community.

The single overriding problem that I see is one
of really getting the act together. There are the
capabilities; there are individual efforts; there
are people within government . . . who have considerable expertise and experience in handling these
episodes. There are resources that can be brought
together to deal effectively with those more
serious episodes. . . .

We don't have the machinery, the focal point
for bringing these capabilities together on a
continuing basis.[118]

People can be brought together easily enough to cope with a
major crisis. However, according to Jenkins, there is no
mechanism for assuring their continuing attention to the
problem in the absence of a specific crisis.[119]

Kupperman and Trent have echoed much the same view.
The mechanisms are designed to require inputs by a large
number of individuals and groups not used to working
together on a regular, continuing basis. "They must work in
symphony. If one were to act out of step from the others,
great tragedy might result. Unfortunately, we have had
several bitter lessons."[120] The case of Ambassador Noel in
Khartoum appears to be a relevant one. In that case, the
mistake that seems to have triggered his death and that of
his deputy chief of mission was a public statement by
President Nixon. Since presidents generally do not issue
statements of this kind on their own, someone must have
advised Nixon to issue it while the State Department
negotiator was on his way.

In order for the lead agency concept to work effectively, according to the same writers, it is necessary for
all members of the team to practice working together under

---

[118]Brian M. Jenkins, in An Act to Combat Terrorism,
Hearings, p. 109.

[119]Ibid.

[120]Kupperman and Trent, p. 166.

simulated crises: "Gaming and other such exercises are
needed to maintain a workable lead-agency concept."[121]

The lead agency concept, with its occasionally
fluctuating changes of command, can also produce confusion.
According to Jenkins:

> A recent example of these sorts of problems
> would be the hijacking of the TWA airliner by
> Croatian extremists in September 1976, when accor-
> ding to one Government official who was involved
> in the handling of the episode, the responsibility
> for the action "bounced around the Government like
> a floating crap game." It was not certain who
> would maintain full jurisdiction over the episode.
> The FAA claimed jurisdiction. Because it was an
> American airliner hijacked in the United States,
> the FBI became involved. Once the airliner
> crossed the national frontiers and flew to Canada
> and ultimately France, there was a definite State
> Department involvement. There was, I understand,
> some difficulty in deciding at the moment who
> precisely was making the decisions that had to be
> made.[122]

When the aircraft landed in France, the French government,
of course, assumed full jurisdiction and employed its own
policies and tactics.

The difficulties that ensued between the French and
American governments indicated a major lack of coordination.
As soon as the TWA airliner arrived at Orly Field in Paris,
the French shot out its tires. The French minister of
interior informed the hijackers that their only choices were
to surrender to French authorities and be deported or to be
executed if they threatened the lives of the hostages.
Meanwhile, the Croatian demands for publicity had all been
met, but the American ambassador had a very difficult time
persuading the French to permit him to speak with the hijackers. When he was finally able to do so, and the
hijackers became convinced that their demands had been
printed and distributed, they surrendered and were sent back
to the United States.[123] Added to the chaos within the
United States government was a lack of antecedent consultation and understanding with the French government.

---

[121]Ibid., p. 167.

[122]Brian M. Jenkins, in An Act to Combat Terrorism,
Hearings, p. 108.

[123]New York Times, 13 and 14 September 1976, p. 1.

Within the American government, large numbers of individuals and groups were involved. As soon as the hijacking was reported, L. Douglas Heck, coordinator of the Cabinet Committee to Combat Terrorism, went to his office in the tenth-floor control center of the FAA building in Washington. Transportation Secretary William T. Coleman and FAA Chief John McLucas also soon arrived at the center. Intelligence and logistics experts from the State Department, FAA technical experts, FAA medical advisers, and FAA and State Department psychiatrists were also present. The FAA control center was tied in to the National Security Council by telephone. Meanwhile, the State Department and the Justice Department had established their own task forces. At the scene, the New York Police Department, together with the FBI, had responsibility as long as the plane was on the ground; the FAA became the lead agency once the plane took off; and the State Department assumed the lead role when the plane left American airspace.[124] Coleman and McLucas were both senior to Heck, and the NSC, being closer to the president, would have been difficult to ignore as decisions had to be made. It is understandable that there was "some difficulty in deciding at the moment who precisely was making the decisions that had to be made."[125] Decisions had to be made in the private sector as well; the editor of the New York Times, for example, had to decide whether or not to publish the Croatian manifesto. The government had no legal right to compel him to do so.

Problems of coordination also surface when the terrorist incident is at the local level. Some terrorist crimes do not involve violation of federal laws. In such a case, the local chief of police would have initial jurisdiction, but he might find himself supplanted by higher political authority under some conditions. Where local facilities are inadequate, state law enforcement and political organizations become involved. Formal or informal assistance may be requested from the FBI.[126] No particular problems of this sort have been noted in the literature reviewed, but since they frequently develop in ordinary crime situations, it should be expected that they equally arise where terrorism is concerned.

---

[124]J. Bowyer Bell, A Time of Terror (New York: Basic Books, 1978), p. 9.

[125]Jenkins, in An Act to Combat Terrorism, Hearings, p. 308.

[126]Kelly, in Terrorism, Part 1, Hearings, p. 3075.

Suggested Improvements

Numerous improvements in the federal response structure have been suggested in the literature reviewed. A
representative sampling of these suggestions appears in this
section.

Intelligence and Counterintelligence

Virtually every major work on terrorism emphasizes
the importance of sound, timely intelligence. How best to
collect such intelligence is a profoundly divisive question.
The Reagan administration is currently trying to adopt some
of the intelligence practices of the Nixon administration.
The reaction of liberals, as already mentioned, has been
sharply critical.

One academic student of the intelligence problem has
noted that:

> In this country, there has been a lessening of
> civil liberties for all to catch a few. Many of
> the laws and court orders approving wiretapping,
> "no-knock" searches, entrapment, conspiracy,
> search and seizure have been designed to catch
> organized criminals or "national security risks."
> . . . Whenever government begins to declare war on
> groups, instead of concentrating on activities,
> the means used to deal with groups may become
> imitative of those very groups and can erode other
> civil liberties.[127]

Some writers and political figures argue that a comparatively minor erosion of civil liberties is justified when
the alternative may be the destruction of organized society.
Others regard the cure as worse than the illness.

In this connection, Homer has presented an interesting typology of societal responses to terrorism.
"Inaction" means doing nothing extraordinary about the
problem. "This strategy may be utilized if terror in terms
of material and human losses is very marginal."[128]
"Fatalism" usually means a public admission that it is
either very difficult or even impossible to stop acts of
terror. For instance, if someone is determined to plant a
bomb, there is virtually no way to determine beforehand that
he is going to do it and to stop him from accomplishing his

---

[127]Frederick D. Homer, "Terror in the United States:
Three Perspectives," in The Politics of Terrorism, ed. Michael
Stohl (New York: Marcel Dekker, 1979), p. 393.

[128]Ibid., p. 390.

mission.[129] "Submission" takes place when government is
overwhelmed by terrorism, as was the case in parts of the
early American West. "Deterrence" involves the use of
overwhelming material resources to combat terrorism in order
to give the impression of societal invulnerability.[130] Both
scholars and statesmen have been writing and talking about
terrorism without defining clearly their perception of the
threat and the strategy to be pursued to combat it. Homer
argues that greater clarity of thought and expression is
required if society is to decide how far it wants to go in
collecting intelligence on its own citizens, a very small
fraction of whom may be predisposed to engage in terrorist
acts.

Apart from the sort of intelligence designed to
identify and track suspected terrorists, it seems obvious
from the outpouring of research during the past decade that
a good deal of basic intelligence has been developed.
However, one expert testified before Congress that:

> The Government knows no more now about
> terrorism--skyjacking, kidnapping, and assassina-
> tion, et cetera--than it knew 50 years ago. That
> same statement may still be valid 50 years from
> now.

> The footnote relative to that is: There is no
> systematic approach now extant in this Government
> for collection, storage, retrieval, or analysis of

> relevant data about such crimes. Even the
> intellectual insight that such study is possible
> cannot be discerned in responsible quarters.[131]

Standing in the way of the collection of basic intelligence
on terrorism are "many sacred cows in the Department of
Justice, public attitudes, media conduct, bureaucratic
pressures, and even the Congress itself. . . ."[132] One of
the attitudes that would have to change would be the idea
that the killing or incarceration of a terrorist ends the
incident; in fact, unless he is taken, studied, and under-
stood, and remedial actions are instituted, others will step
into his shoes in due course.

---

[129]Ibid., p. 391.

[130]Ibid., p. 392.

[131]David Hubbard, in Terrorism, Part 1, Hearings,
p. 2976.

[132]Ibid.

A great deal of intelligence amassed within the United States government is not distributed to those who may encounter terrorism in the course of their law enforcement duties. "The CIA has access to vast stores of information that could affect the operations of a local law enforcement agency."[133] However, there is no way that information can be conveyed, under present law, to state and local law enforcement officials. Information developed on kidnapping methods used in Argentina, for example, could provide valuable insights for domestic law enforcement agencies. "Just as we have mass transportation information on a very rapid basis, that kind of feedback from the international sector could be of assistance to us."[134]

There should be no direct contact between the CIA and local law enforcement agencies, according to Kelly. When the CIA tried to provide training in guerrilla tactics being used in other countries, there was a public outcry when the media found out about it and reported it. Therefore, the dissemination of information would have to be through some other organization such as the Department of State or the Department of Justice.

Another problem mentioned by a number of witnesses was the flow of intelligence from state and local law enforcement agencies to federal agencies. Because of the Freedom of Information Act, many local police departments who may have some information about terrorist groups are reluctant to share it with federal agencies. Should the information they have developed come into the public domain, they would be embarrassed and their efforts jeopardized.

Another intelligence problem has been identified as that of effecting communication between domestic and foreign police agencies dealing with intelligence concerning terrorism.

> The FBI does play an important role in helping to communicate between the various law enforcement agencies on the international scene. But you must bear in mind that the FBI is primarily a domestic agency. Interpol has an excellent reputation but it is a small unit, and it is represented in the United States by someone in the Treasury Department. This is really outside the mainstream of law enforcement as it is established today.

---

[133]Kelly, in _Terrorism, Part 1_, Hearings, p. 3062.

[134]Ibid.

> In my opinion, the representative should be
> under the Attorney General of the United States,
> so that Interpol could be coordinated with the
> total flow of law enforcement.[135]

In other words, a more effective method should be devised to
make certain that relevant information about international
terrorism is brought to the attention of all interested
domestic antiterrorist organizations. In the view of this
particular observer, that role should be played by the
Department of Justice.

Very little information of value regarding the
quality of intelligence developed from local and foreign
sources and by different groups and agencies is found in the
available literature. Professional courtesy appears to
preclude criticism from those in a position to judge the
product. Outsiders cannot be expected to have a fair sample
of the intelligence product from which to draw valid
conclusions. There are indications, however, that something
must be wrong with the system when information available to
the FBI--regarding Lee Harvey Oswald, for example--was not
conveyed to those authorities responsible for protecting
President Kennedy.[136] The man who tried to assassinate
President Reagan had been turned back at an airport after
trying to board a plane with two handguns in his possession.
On the other hand, the Black Panthers, who were decimated by
law enforcement agencies, were extreme in their rhetoric and
provocative in their actions but probably not terrorists.[137]

Since it is not acknowledged by the experts that the
quality of intelligence leaves something to be desired,
there are no suggestions concerning how to obtain better
intelligence and analysis. The usual plea is for a freer
hand for the domestic intelligence agencies to engage in
electronic surveillance and to use informants. One example
is the argument of Cooper:

> While the use of espionage, internationally, is
> at least more palatable to a majority, the use of
> intelligence, counter-intelligence and the develop-
> ment of the sort of preventive intelligence capa-
> bility that is necessary to take effective measures
> against domestic terrorism still sticks in the craw

---

[135]Ibid.

[136]President's Commission on the Assassination of
President Kennedy, Report (Washington, D.C.: Government
Printing Office, 1964), pp. 29-30, 429-44.

[137]Albert Parry, Terrorism: From Robespierre to
Arafat (New York: Vanguard Press, 1976), pp. 301-21.

of many. That there have been mismanagement and excesses in this area is unquestionable. That many whose activities can hardly be described as criminal have suffered intrusions upon their privacy and even harassment cannot be denied. None of this can, however, be made the foundation for an attack upon the development of a properly controlled preventive intelligence gathering capacity.[138]

There is very little discussion in the professional law enforcement literature about how intelligence and counter-intelligence are to be properly controlled. Moreover, it is assumed, but not demonstrated, that the lifting of restraints on political intelligence gathering will result in an improved intelligence product.

The Policy of No Concessions

The arguments for and against a policy of no concessions have been discussed in the context of criticism of current American policy. Essentially, that policy is based on the assumption that "to prevent further attacks, one must not give in to what the [terrorists] demand; thus one makes future operations not worth their while."[139] Two alternative positions have been advocated.

One alternative would be a tougher policy still, more akin to the Israeli "eye for an eye" posture. President Reagan appears to be leaning in that direction. A State Department statement of February 19, 1981, declared that "the present administration would not have negotiated with Iran for the release of the hostages. Future acts of state-sponsored terrorism against the United States will meet swift and sure punishment."[140] President Ford's action against the Cambodian captors of the Mayaguez may be an example of what Reagan had in mind, but neither he nor Secretary of State Haig have ever been specific about the form the contemplated punishment would take. The Israelis have repeatedly made it clear through deeds, not words, that the hostages might be sacrificed but that the terrorists

---

[138]H. H. A. Cooper, "Terrorism and the Intelligence Function," in Contemporary Terrorism: Selected Readings, ed. John D. Elliott and Leslie K. Gibson (Gaithersburg, Md.: International Association of Chiefs of Police, 1978), p. 188.

[139]Mickolus, p. 312.

[140]Cited in Evans and Novak, p. 196.

would surely be killed. The United States has had a similarly tough policy in theory, but has usually placed first priority on the lives of hostages. Moreover, as far as can be determined, there has been no attempt by the United States to track down and kill terrorist assassins abroad. The people who murdered Ambassador Noel in Khartoum are still alive. The Israelis, with only a fraction of the American capabilities in covert action, would not have permitted the assassins to live.

The other alternative is to adopt a flexible policy that places the lives of the hostages first. In the case of domestic kidnappings, ransom is usually paid. Once the victim is free, however, the kidnappers are usually caught by the FBI and punished by the judicial system. The same posture could be adopted by the government for international hostage and kidnapping incidents. Moreover:

> The contagion hypothesis rests on shaky evidence. At present, we are unable to test whether terrorist groups are aware of "no ransom" policies or whether they base their behavior on knowledge of such policies. Furthermore, many governments have publicly stated beforehand their refusal to deal with groups who take hostages, yet have been faced with incidents on their soil involving their nationals as perpetrators or as targets. Such nations include Argentina, Israel, Turkey, Uruguay, West Germany, and Japan, not to mention the United States.[141]

Furthermore, it could be argued that a government which sends virtually defenseless diplomats on peaceful missions overseas is morally bound to see to it that their safety is assured by a flexible policy. Once the hostages have been released, retaliation can follow, either by the host government or by American agents.

Not all terrorist groups are alike. "Resort to radical action may be the only way these individuals can articulate their interests."[142] Those people who lost their health and homes at Love Canal in New York state and found government completely unresponsive to their needs might well have resorted to terrorism to gain the attention of politicians.[143] They would have been in a different category from the groups that deliberately set out to destroy the form of

---

[141]Mickolus, p. 216.

[142]Ibid., p. 217.

[143]Joanne Omang, "Stirrings of Life Return to Love Canal," Washington Post, 9 November 1981, pp. A-1, A-2.

government that a majority of the American people appears to
want. A flexible policy permits government to make necessary distinctions. Each incident can be managed in order to
minimize the damage to individuals and to the social order
in general.

Mickolus has suggested that one alternative policy
would be to make it clear to the terrorists that the government places humanitarian considerations first. If the
terrorists appear to be the oppressors, while the government
is the one that demonstrates a high regard for human life
and liberties, the terrorists will have lost the psychological and political advantages for which they undertook the
action in the first place.[144] A policy of this kind can
only be expected to work under certain conditions, with some
types of terrorists, and if a flexible policy has been
adopted. For instance, where the terrorism is part of a war
to the death between rival ideologies, a "humanitarian
policy" toward negotiations or ransom might be taken as a
sign of weakness by the terrorists and would probably fail
to improve the political climate or to save the government.

The Response Mechanism

Expert witnesses before various congressional
committees have primarily emphasized the need for extending
assistance to state and local law enforcement officials
required to deal with terrorism. Many terrorist acts can
fall exclusively within the jurisdiction of state and local
governments, which may not have the expertise to be found at
the federal law enforcement level. Only eight and one-half
percent of all employees in the criminal justice system are
employed by the federal government.[145]

Dr. Hacker, a psychiatrist with experience in
hostage and kidnapping cases, suggested the formulation of
special teams to assist state and local law enforcement
officials.

. . . All over the country each local police
force or law enforcement agency that has the
responsibility of solving a case that happens in
its jurisdiction, should be privileged to have
the advice of . . . teams either on the spot or
by telephone or whatnot, teams which have been
properly trained. It should be obligatory that
whoever makes the decision about these matters

---

[144]Mickolus, p. 220.

[145]Richard W. Velde, in Terrorism, Part 4, Hearings,
p. 4136.

has to consult with that team. It does not necessarily have to take the advice of that team--that would be too much of an interference in that structure--but every police chief or whoever makes that type of decision should be obligated to consult with a team of that sort.[146]

The "teams" would be regional study and action groups representing various disciplines. Included in each team would be a member of the FBI, criminologists, psychiatrists, and media analysts, together with representatives of other disciplines who might be able to make useful contributions. Whenever an important terrorist act was committed anywhere in the United States, one of these teams would be convened immediately, providing the capacity to render such assistance as might be required.

In a later submission to the committee, Hacker suggested that among the other disciplines to be represented should be sociology, linguistics, and cultural anthropology. The regional teams should be established by and be responsible to the federal response mechanism. A permanent staff should control and coordinate the teams, with regular meetings in Washington to share insights and information. Members of a team should be given security clearances of the sort that would enable them to have access to all relevant materials and intelligence.

There should be no delay between research and action-type thinking. I believe, in general, one of the bad things of modern research has been the isolation of the doers who do not think very much and the thinkers who do not do very much and the twain never meet. We do not want one group of people who have all the information but cannot do anything about it and the other group who has all the power to act, yet doesn't know anything [147]

Members of the teams should be the best ones that can be found anywhere in the nation in their respective fields. Since the members are likely to be busy individuals, alternates would have to be appointed.

James Kelly of the International Association of Chiefs of Police endorsed the idea of special advisory teams, but carried it one step further. He believed that such teams should be established in the major cities and in each state.

---

[146]Frederick J. Hacker, in Terrorism, Part 1, Hearings, p. 3011.

[147]Ibid., p. 3028.

The Federal level in that case could provide a corps, a permanent corps within, say, the Justice Department, who would have some people who could conduct research and an ongoing process of investigating these cases. This could encompass analyzing the news media on an international basis.[148]

In addition, it should be possible to develop contingency plans which would include groups of experts in a variety of research and operational fields. When the need arose, these experts, whether commandos or sociologists, would be drafted to help in a particular terrorist incident. The same experts could also be used to train federal, state, and local law enforcement personnel.[149]

Although the idea of multidisciplinary study and action teams was endorsed enthusiastically by a number of witnesses and by Chairman Ichord of Missouri, nothing ever came of it.

Very little emerged regarding the chain-of-command system in the United States. On most occasions, either the local chief of police or the FBI agent-in-charge has primary responsibility. However, neat organizational arrangements which sound good on paper may not work in practice because "there is so much emotionalism--police officers are affected by what is going on around them."[150] If local police are to defer to the FBI, it is necessary that this possibility be emphasized during their training and reemphasized again and again.

The possibility was also raised during the various congressional hearings that terrorists might acquire and use, or threaten to use, powerful and sophisticated weapons with which state and local law enforcement agencies could not hope to cope. In such cases, assistance would have to come from the military. No contingency plans for assistance of this nature existed. In an emergency, the law enforcement official in charge would not know where to turn to receive the required help in time to correct the existing situation.[151] The witness believed that it was essential for such contingency plans to be drafted and kept up to date.

---

[148]James Kelly, in ibid., p. 3064.

[149]Ibid.

[150]Ibid., p. 3075.

[151]Robert L. Rabe, in Terrorism, Part 2, Hearings, p. 3226.

Another suggestion regarding the use of the military was made during a more recent set of congressional hearings. If the size and sophistication of terrorist activity overwhelmed federal, state, and local law enforcement agencies, the president, upon the advice of the attorney general, could call in the military. The military would act in accordance with constraints and limits established by civilian authority, but would be under the tactical control of the military commander. Congressman Seiberling, having in mind the Kent State incident, suggested that some provision be made for retaining control by the responsible civilian law enforcement officer on the scene. He was informed that such a procedure could not be envisaged under existing law.[152]

The existence of "a specially trained [U.S. Army] unit for overseas use in high-risk situations involving American citizens" was mentioned during the congressional hearings.[153] The name "Delta Force" was provided to the Congress but no details were given in public session. This unit formed the nucleus of the team that attempted rescuing the American hostages in Iran. However, it was augmented at the last moment by personnel from the Navy and the Marine Corps, a factor which caused considerable confusion and friction and which may have contributed to the mission's failure.[154]

At all of the congressional hearings investigating the federal response to terrorism, the usual procedure was for administration witnesses to explain the mechanisms and measures that had been established. Senators and congressmen asked questions about the mechanism only to clarify the witnesses' statements, but made no suggestions about what might be done to improve it. The one exception was Father Drinan of Massachusetts, who suggested that the federal government, with all its elaborate coordinating mechanisms, was merely "spinning its wheels," since no one had been able to solve the bombing of the Capitol and the bombing of the baggage room at La Guardia Airport. Although he appeared to imply that the entire structure might just as well be

---

[152]John E. Seiberling, "Question," in _Federal Capabilities in Crisis Management and Terrorism_, Hearings Before the Subcommittee on Civil and Constitutional Rights, House of Representatives, 95th Congress, 2nd Sess. (Washington, D.C.: Government Printing Office, 1978), p. 48.

[153]Ibid., p. 50.

[154]Drew Middleton, "Going the Military Route," _New York Times Magazine_, Special Edition, 1981, p. 108.

discarded, he made no specific suggestions concerning how it might be rebuilt or improved.[155]

At various times, Congress considered legislative measures to improve American performance in the fight against international terrorism. The Treasury Department's Bureau of Alcohol, Tobacco, and Firearms (BATF) recommended that Congress enact legislation requiring manufacturers of black and smokeless gunpowders to identify each batch with a special "taggant." This proposal was deemed to be impractical by the National Rifle Association. Because such powders are normally produced in lots of ten to 20 thousand pounds but sold at retail in one-half-pound and one-pound canisters, it would be technically impossible to identify each particular canister and the presumed bomber. Moreover, the dynamite and blasting caps normally used by terrorists for bombings are almost invariably stolen, and such materials as ammonium nitrate (a fertilizer) and gasoline can be used to make even more powerful bombs than those constructed with gunpowders or dynamite.[156] The proposed measure has still not been enacted.

Another suggestion was to make it mandatory for the administration to cut off all trade with countries such as Libya that support terrorism. Various administration spokesmen indicated that such legislation would not be helpful, primarily because it would restrict freedom of action, and it was not enacted into law.[157]

Turning to suggestions from unofficial sources, President Carter established a new agency on June 19, 1978, to deal with civil emergency preparedness. As established, the agency would act only after a major terrorist act had devastated an area of the United States. Its primary function was to handle the federal responsibility for dealing with all natural and man-made disasters, including nuclear attack. It has been suggested that this agency

---

[155]Robert F. Drinan, in _Federal Capabilities in Crisis Management and Terrorism_, Hearings, pp. 67-68.

[156]Neal Knox, "Testimony," in _Omnibus Antiterrorism Act of 1979_, Hearings Before the Committee on Governmental Affairs, Senate, 96th Congress, 1st Sess. (Washington, D.C.: Government Printing Office, 1979), pp. 138-47.

[157]Lester L. Wolff, "Comments," in _International Terrorism: Legislative Initiatives_, Hearings Before the Committee on International Relations, House of Representatives, 95th Congress, 2nd Sess. (Washington, D.C.: Government Printing Office, 1978), p. 120.

could play a major role in planning for the consequences of terrorist attacks.[158]

> The need for a truly effective preparedness program on the federal level has never been greater, and we submit that a critical mass of experts is preferable to the kind of ad hoc bureaucratic shuffle that has been experienced during the last five years. It is obvious that the crisis management structure . . . can operate most effectively with clear and comprehensive authority delegated from a strong Chief Executive. The relationship between dealing with the terrorist incident and mitigating its consequences needs to be carefully thought out.[159]

Bell takes a dim view of the existing federal response mechanism but offers only an indirect solution.

> . . . Even arrangements at the center are more form than substance. In the United States, the Cabinet Committee to Combat Terrorism met only a few times after 1972. The Working Group of the Committee represents twenty-six departments, but the representation is often by officials with little if any bureaucratic leverage. The group is a coordinating body, not a control center. The Department of State's Office for Combating Terrorism has five officials and two secretaries. Ambassador Heck, State's representative on the Cabinet Committee in 1966-1977, and one more in a string of appointments to the post, left in 1977 to become Ambassador to Nepal, some indication of State's priorities.[160]

Bell points out that since these coordinating mechanisms have no control authority, decisions tend to be made by the NSC or in the Oval Office, particularly if the terrorist incident is viewed as politically important. Contingency planning remains inadequate after nearly a decade of efforts along these lines. Bell seems to be arguing for a command and control center at a high enough level to make decisions. As a practical matter, such a center would probably have to be located somewhere within the NSC or White House structure.

---

[158]Kupperman and Trent, pp. 168-71.

[159]Ibid., p. 177.

[160]Bell, p. 270.

Within the response structure, it seems generally to be agreed that attention needs to be paid to the public relations aspect of terrorism. Terrorism depends on the media:

> The prospect of standing alone for a moment upon the stage of world history is fatally attractive to many tormented minds. . . . But organized terrorism has truly made television its own and, in consequence, as a manifestation of our times it has become larger than life, more dreadful than would ever have been possible without the medium.[161]

A major terrorist act enables the terrorists literally to capture the most powerful medium the world has ever known. During the March, 1975, kidnapping of West Berlin mayoral candidate Peter Lorenz, the Baader-Meinhof Gang dictated the programming of American as well as German television stations.[162] The Iranian hostage crisis in the period before American television crews were expelled from Iran represented an even more flagrant "rape" of the media. A CIA research study indicated that whenever a terrorist's goals included gaining major publicity, there was virtually a 100 percent probability that the goal would be achieved.[163] Certain types of terrorism might well not exist if the world had not become unified via television and communication satellites. Most of the congressional witnesses and the literature agree that anything that can be done to curb media appetite for the sensational would be a help in stemming the terrorist tide. In the words of Evans, "An American policy to strengthen deterrence of hostage situations is to delegitimize hostage taking as a tactic for revolutionary groups."[164] Media specialists, therefore, need to play a larger role than they have to date in the federal response structure. In the light of constitutional

---

[161]H. H. A. Cooper, "Terrorism and the Media," in Terrorism: Interdisciplinary Perspectives, ed. Yonah Alexander and Seymour Maxwell Finger (New York: John Jay Press, 1977), p. 144.

[162]Melvin J. Lasky, "Ulrike Meinhof and the Baader-Meinhof Gang," Encounter 44 (June 1975):15-16.

[163]Davis Milbank, International and Transnational Terrorism: Diagnosis and Prognosis (Washington, D.C.: Central Intelligence Agency, April 1976), p. 22.

[164]Ernest Evans, Calling a Truce to Terror: The American Response to International Terrorism (Westport, Conn.: Greenwood Press, 1979), p. 117.

provisions, these specialists would undoubtedly have to proceed by persuasion rather than by law or coercion.[165]

Response Structures of Other Nations

Before turning to the response structures of other nations, that adopted by the New York City Police Department (NYPD) merits examination. The NYPD structure and tactics have been used as a model throughout the world. Since the program's inception in 1973, following the Munich massacre, the NYPD has never lost a hostage, a police officer, or even a perpetrator.[166]

The operation against the Israeli athletes at the Munich Olympics in September, 1972, shocked the world and galvanized the U.S. government into developing its response structure to cope with possible terrorist threats. It also sparked action in New York City, headquarters of the United Nations, with delegates likely to become targets of terrorism. The commanding officer of the Special Operations Division of the NYPD promptly summoned representatives of the Police Academy, the Emergency Service Unit, and the Detective Bureau, and the chief of the Psychological Services Section. The group developed guidelines spelling out the responsibilities of the various parts of the department. The basic strategy followed is to contain and negotiate rather than attempt to use force. Detectives of the department specially trained in psychology and other skills do all the negotiating because it is believed that they will be more likely to remain unafraid and calm under pressure than would negotiators from other groups. The detective-negotiators speak virtually all of the languages that might be useful, including Croatian and Arabic. All have received training in jurisdictional matters, including relations with the FBI and the FAA. It is an invariable rule that the patrol borough commander remains in charge of the entire operation from start to finish. He and not the mayor or the chief of police makes the important decisions.

---

[165]"Terrified of Television," _Economist_ (London), 22 March 1980, p. 59.

[166]Francis A. Bolz, Jr., "Hostage Confrontation and Rescue," in _Terrorism: Threat, Reality, Response_, ed. Robert Kupperman and Darrell Trent (Stanford, Calif.: Hoover Institution Press of Stanford University, 1979), p. 393.

The reason for this command framework is that the senior officer who is most familiar with the locality involved will be able to make more knowledgeable decisions. He will also be left to deal with the community when the Speciality Units pack up their "hardware" and move on.[167]

The principle of control by the most senior and experienced officer in the borough is worth underlining, because it is the antithesis of the method of command used at the federal level. In any administration, the most senior people--president, cabinet officers, and senior NSC personnel--are political leaders or political appointees. They take advice from the most senior and experienced officers--the country director for the Sudan in the case of the Khartoum kidnapping, for example--but it is they who make the decisions, not the experts.

Israel

The NYPD strategy is also the opposite of that used by Israel, certainly one of the countries that has had the greatest experience with terrorism. The Israelis never negotiate, even when the hostages' lives must all be forfeited as at Munich; they use deadly force on the spot, whenever possible; and when the immediate application of deadly force is not possible, they carry out a policy of reprisals.[168] Part of this policy stems from Israel's geopolitical situation as a small enclave in an area of hostile nations, and part from the fate of Jews in Europe during World War II.

Between 1949 and 1953, there were frequent raids into Israel by Palestinian refugees seeking revenge for the loss of their homeland. The Israelis invariably responded with countering military raids aimed at the villages in Jordan and Lebanon from which the Palestinian raiders had come. These raids were never acknowledged by the Israeli government.

Beginning in 1953, Army Chief of Staff Moshe Dayan developed, and the Israeli cabinet approved, a new policy. A special "101" military unit was trained to carry out reprisals, and it was decided that, in order to be effective, several Arabs would have to be killed for each Israeli victimized. Reprisals were now publicly acknowledged.[169]

---

[167]Ibid., p. 396.

[168]Ernest Evans, p. 119.

[169]Ibid.

From this point on, there was a gradual escalation of the Israeli reprisal policy. As Palestinian raids continued, the policy was broadened to cause pain and suffering to those Arab governments providing sanctuary and other assistance to the Palestinians. Beginning around 1967, the Israelis moved beyond punitive raids into the realm of full military activity directed against Palestinian bases in Lebanon, Jordan, and elsewhere.[170]

One American student of the Israeli policy concluded that the raids did serve as something of a deterrent for a limited period of time. Punitive action directed against neighboring Arab governments appeared to result in a diminution of raids against Israel for periods of up to a month, but then they would start up again.[171]

Such a policy would not be feasible for the United States. Israel is technically in a state of war with all of its Arab neighbors except Egypt. Periodically, the reprisal policy has led to an escalation of "international tensions to such a degree that war may result. The Israeli reprisals in 1955-1956 and in 1965-1967, for example, were a major factor in the escalation process that led to the 1956 and 1967 Middle East wars."[172] The policy has alienated other nations as well; France placed a total embargo on its shipments of arms and spare parts to Israel following the Israeli raid on Beirut's airport.[173] The United States has also held up shipments of arms to Israel following some particularly dramatic instance of the reprisal policy. Israel has been condemned by a number of United Nations bodies, including the General Assembly.

The Israeli success in the Entebbe raid was unusual. In most instances, the Israeli hard-line policy has resulted in the deaths of many or even all of the hostages. In the case of the Munich Olympians, the Israeli government refused to accede to the terrorists' demands--the release of Arab prisoners in Israeli jails--and demanded that the German government not permit the Israeli athletes to be taken out

---

[170]Ibid.

[171]Barry Blechman, "The Impact of Israel's Reprisals on Behavior of the Bordering Arab Nations Directed at Israel," Journal of Conflict Resolution 16 (June 1972):155-81.

[172]Ernest Evans, p. 121.

[173]Barry Blechman, "The Consequences of Israeli Reprisals: An Assessment" (Ph.D. dissertation, Georgetown University, 1971), p. 214.

of the country. Following the attempt by the German police to free the hostages, all nine of them were killed.[174]

The Israeli response structure is similar to that which would prevail in most countries in wartime, with the exception that each operation appears to be presented to and approved by the prime minister after consultation with the cabinet.[175] However, Israel is a small country always on a war footing. The characteristics and capabilities of military and civilian personnel are well known to those in power. Even so, Israeli policy has not been notably successful in curbing the terrorist threat.

Canada

Canada's situation is similar to that of the United States. There is a common dedication to democratic forms of government, a geographical proximity, and a roughly comparable federal structure. Beginning in 1963, Quebecois separatists began using terrorist tactics to achieve their goal of a separate "French" nation inside or outside the Canadian federation. The police enjoyed considerable success in arresting terrorists and even in eliminating entire organizations, but new recruits and groups kept the region in ferment. On June 24, 1970, a bomb exploded at defense headquarters in Ottawa, killing one person; and on October 5, 1970, the British trade commissioner in Montreal was kidnapped by four armed members of the Quebec Liberation Front (FLQ). October 10 saw the kidnapping of Pierre Laporte, minister of labor and manpower, minister of immigration, and house leader of the Quebec government. These events ushered in the "October Crisis."[176]

On October 16, 1970, the federal government proclaimed the War Measures Act for the first time while the nation was at peace. Under this law, preventive detention was permitted and the FLQ was outlawed. The federal cabinet was provided with unrestricted authority to make orders and

---

[174]Bolz, p. 395.

[175]Liston, p. 129.

[176]Brian A. Grosman, "Dissent and Disorder in Canada," in Disorders and Terrorism: Report of the Task Force on Disorders and Terrorism (Washington, D.C.: National Advisory Committee on Criminal Justice Standards and Goals, 1976), pp. 479-89.

regulations to deal with the emergency. On October 17, the day after these emergency measures were invoked, the dead body of Minister Laporte was found. On the other hand, Cross, the British trade commissioner, was found and freed. Hundreds of members of the FLQ were arrested, including those responsible for Laporte's kidnapping and murder. These police measures, together with the public outrage over the murder of Laporte, served to break the back of the illegal separatist movement.[177]

The ability of the federal government to take over in response to serious terrorist or other attacks enables it to suspend constitutional guarantees and to cut through jurisdictional lines. Yet, many Canadians are disturbed that the War Measures Act remains Canada's "only legislative response, outside the criminal code provisions, to apprehend insurrection, terrorist violence, and major civil disorder."[178]

The United Kingdom

Britain's principal terrorist problem is the result of the partition of Ireland in 1929. The 26 Catholic-dominated counties in the south received independence, while the six counties in the north with Protestant majorities remained tied to Britain. Since 1969, terrorism and urban guerrilla warfare have been waged by both the Irish Republican Army's Provisional Wing and Protestant extremists, against each other, against the British forces in Northern Ireland, and against British targets everywhere in the United Kingdom, including London. Most Catholics in Ulster want unification with the Republic of Ireland but do not approve of the Provisional Wing's tactics. The Protestant majority, and in particular the militant Ulster Defense Association, would resist unification by force. The British government has been caught in the middle for more than a decade of bloodletting.[179]

One of the most recent tactics of the IRA was a hunger strike, for the purposes of forcing the British government to accord political status to imprisoned members of the organization. The British government refused to

---

[177]Ibid., pp. 490-91.

[178]Ibid., p. 491.

[179]David Reed, "Northern Ireland--the Endless War," Reader's Digest, July 1975, pp. 84-93.

change its stance despite the deaths of ten hunger strikers,
and the tactic ended in failure.[180]

The British government has repeatedly attempted to
negotiate a settlement. However, the Provisional IRA has
sabotaged every settlement offer, including the 1979 Fitz-
gerald plan. This plan:

> . . . seemed to be favored by both the govern-
> ment and opposition parties in the Irish Republic,
> Ulster's moderate Protestants and Catholics, the
> British government, and the Irish-American Estab-
> lishment headed by the Kennedy family clan. The
> Provisional IRA's response to that intolerable
> threat was to blow up Lord Mountbatten on his
> fishing boat in Donegal Bay.[181]

Mountbatten had not been involved in politics since retiring
as the last British ruler of India a quarter of a century
earlier; his death was engineered merely to cause the Fitz-
gerald plan to fail.

In fighting the Provisional IRA, the British have
some constitutional advantages that the United States does
not possess. British sovereignty resides in Parliament,
which is controlled by the majority party. Parliament can
make or unmake any law without restrictions. Prime Minister
Thatcher was apparently directly involved in the decision
not to give in to the hunger strikers. Day-to-day developments are the responsibility of the secretary of state for
Northern Ireland. Policy is established by the prime
minister with the advice of the entire cabinet.[182]

While continuing to seek grounds for negotiation,
the British have tried to scale down their military presence
in Northern Ireland. Their troop strength has been cut from
22,000 in 1972 to under 12,000 in 1981, while the indigenous
Ulster Defense Regiment has grown from 700 to 3,000 and the
local police forces have increased from 4,000 to 7,000.
Eventually, the people of Northern Ireland may develop the
means to cope with the Provisional IRA by themselves.[183]

---

[180]Bob Levin, with Lea Donosky, "Death Wish in
Ulster," Newsweek, 4 May 1981, pp. 40-41; idem, "Ulster's
Days of Rage," Newsweek, 11 May 1981, pp. 38-41.

[181]Sterling, The Terror Network, pp. 167-68.

[182]Bob Levin, with Lea Donosky, "The Legacy of Bobby
Sands," Newsweek, 18 May 1981, pp. 50-53.

[183]Ibid.

The campaign against the Provisional IRA has caused a variety of human rights problems. The allegation that IRA prisoners were being tortured raised a storm of protest.[184]

West Germany

West Germany has been plagued by terrorism of relatively modest dimensions compared to Canada and Great Britain. Even so, such comparatively small groups as the Baader-Meinhof Gang and the July 2nd Movement have perpetrated some spectacular terrorist acts, including the assassination of the chief justice of the highest court in Berlin and the Lorenz kidnapping. Abroad, there was the abortive raid on the West German embassy in Stockholm in the spring of 1975. There have been sporadic attacks against American installations in West Germany. Initially, the Germans were hampered by a federalism that posed problems similar to those in the United States.

German success in dealing with terrorism was partly due to its strengthening of the federal police force, the Bundeskriminalamt, an organization somewhat comparable to the FBI. A law enacted September 19, 1971, gave this group more executive powers. These powers were augmented further in June, 1973. The Bundeskriminalamt was given yet increased executive powers and the responsibility for maintaining and disseminating centralized information concerning terrorism and related activities. A computerized and centralized recordkeeping system was established on all known criminals and criminal activities.[185]

The federal police role was further increased by giving it jurisdiction over a number of crimes formerly the responsibility of the individual German states. Those categories of crimes made the responsibility of the Bundeskriminalamt included internationally organized illicit traffic in weaponry, ammunitions, explosives, drugs, and false currency, crimes committed against certain high officers of the government and their guests, and all cases involving the diplomatic corps. The federal police force also assumes jurisdiction whenever state authorities request

---

[184]Joseph W. Bishop, Jr., "Law in the Control of Terrorism and Insurrection: The British Laboratory Experience," Law and Contemporary Problems 42 (Spring 1978): 140-202.

[185]Herman Blei, "Terrorism, Domestic and International: The West German Experience," in Disorders and Terrorism: Report of the Task Force on Disorders and Terrorism (Washington, D.C.: National Advisory Committee on Criminal Justice Standards and Goals, 1976), p. 505.

its aid, if the federal minister of the interior so directs, or if the federal chief prosecutor orders it to intervene in any cases which he is investigating. In effect, the federal force has superseded state and local police forces in all cases involving terrorism. To cope with these responsibilities, it has been greatly expanded, and a special section dealing with terrorism has been created.[186]

In addition, the German social-science establishment has devoted a good deal of attention to the phenomenon of terrorism. German scholarship tends to look at the terrorist in a social context rather than as an aberrant individual.[187] This tendency is attributable to the fact that psychiatric examination of members of the Baader-Meinhof Gang revealed no symptoms of neurosis or psychosis.

The German response structure appears marked by the absence of conflicting jurisdictions. The federal responsibility for fighting terrorism is accepted by the states. Within the federal structure, the minister of the interior has general responsibility for all measures to combat terrorism, subject to possible overruling by the cabinet.

Turkey

Few nations have experienced as massive an attack by terrorists as has Turkey. In addition to politically motivated domestic terrorism by both right and left, there have been attacks on Turks and Turkish interests by Greek Cypriots and by Armenians. As a result, Claire Sterling wrote in 1981 of "the great strategic landmass of Turkey lying prostrate, ungoverned and ungovernable, a terminal case."[188]

Political terrorism began to plague Turkey in 1975. Since then, the toll in lives has steadily mounted: there were 2 murders in 1976, 231 in 1977, 832 in 1978, and 1,200 in 19 9. Political assassinations were running at the rate of 2, 00 in 1980. Among the victims in July, 1980, were three prominent politicians, including a former president and a deputy in the Parliament.[189] Much of the terrorism

---

[186]Ibid., pp. 499, 505.

[187]Constance Holden, "Study of Terrorism Emerging as an International Endeavor," Science 203 (5 January 1979):33-35.

[188]Sterling, The Terror Network, p. 295.

[189]"Can the Turks Unite Against Terror?" Economist (London), 26 July 1980, pp. 45-46.

appeared to be a contest of strength between the Marxist extreme left and the Islamic far right. Essentially, terrorism spread very rapidly in Turkey "not because the terrorists were so strong but because the government was so weak, and because the terrorists received considerable support from the outside."[190] The government was weak primarily because neither of the major political parties could gain a parliamentary majority or would agree to cooperate. "By 1979, large sections of Turkey were divided into liberated areas in which one of the armed camps established more or less complete control."[191] Sterling's description of Turkey as a terminal case appeared all too accurate.

In September, 1980, however, the Turkish army assumed control and quickly decimated the terrorists. It also boosted lagging industrial production by devaluing the Turkish lira and by outlawing strikes. Terrorism, extortion, and political violence were brought under control very soon after the September 12 takeover. Hundreds of known terrorists were arrested. The death penalty was reinstated; two men convicted of terrorist killings in Ankara were hanged days after a military court passed sentence on them. An attempt by terrorists to hijack a Turkish Airlines plane in Diyarbakir in October was met by an armed response which resulted in the capture of all four terrorists. Moreover, the military has moved against terrorism from both leftist and rightist factions; under the civilian governments it had always been alleged that favoritism was being shown one side or another. The military, and not the police, became the principal antiterrorist force. The military leaders have also made it clear that they intend to remain in power until the "anarchy" has been overcome and the country "cleaned up."[192]

These dramatic improvements were achieved at a cost in civil liberties. For example, workers who stage work slowdowns are considered traitors and may be sentenced to prison terms. Military courts have superseded civil courts for all cases involving matters of public order.[193]

---

[190]Walter Laqueur, "Turkey's Trials," New Republic, 11 October 1980, p. 14.

[191]Ibid., p. 15.

[192]Metin Demirsar, "Turkey's Generals Curb Terrorism," Wall Street Journal, 17 October 1980, p. 35.

[193]Ibid.

Italy

Italy has struggled with terrorism for more than a decade, with some successes and many failures. The most significant terrorist coup was the kidnapping and murder of Aldo Moro, Italy's senior political leader, in March, 1978. Moro was a key figure in Italian politics because he had succeeded in keeping his Christian Democratic Party in power by enlisting the support of the Italian Communist Party. He was kidnapped on the day that this union promised Italy a measure of political stability by inaugurating a new coalition government. The government took extraordinary measures--employment of additional police methods--but was unable to locate Moro or his kidnappers.[194]

In May, 1980, Italian police captured three members of the Red Brigades who had just assassinated a Christian Democratic politician. One of the assassins was Patrizio Peci, the leader of the Turin group of the Red Brigades. He was persuaded to talk, and the police were able to use the information given them virtually to wipe out the Turin and Genoa "columns" of the Red Brigades.[195]

Elsewhere in Italy, however, it was "business as usual" for the terrorists. In July, 1981, for example, the Red Brigades kidnapped Patrizio Peci's younger brother Roberti, threatening to kill him unless the police agreed to exchange him for his brother. A chemical company executive was murdered after the terrorists' demands were refused. Ciro Cirillo, a Christian Democratic politician and an official of the nationalized Alfa-Romero car company, was being held by the Red Brigades in Rome under the sentence of death.[196] Numerous additional examples could be cited. Until recently, the Italian government has been unable to develop a suitable response mechanism to cope with terrorism. Unlike Germany, Italy will not negotiate with terrorists.[197]

---

[194]Blackstone Reports, "Terrorism in Italy: A New Dimension," Security Management, November 1978, pp. 42-43.

[195]John Brecher, with Loren Jenkins, "Joining Forces Against Terrorism," Newsweek, 2 June 1980, p. 50.

[196]Associated Press, "Red Brigades Sentence Victim to Death," Dallas Morning News, 11 July 1981, p. 3.

[197]Associated Press, "Italy Won't Talk with Terrorists," New York Times, 14 July 1981, p. 3.

Western Europe

A major weapon in the war against terrorism in Western Europe has been a high level of cooperation among national police forces.

> . . . police all across Europe are sharing information and resources. At the heart of this effort is the powerful central computer of the German police; it contains the names of thousands of suspects, including terrorists. This data bank is supplemented by a constant exchange of across-the-border tips and an old-boy network of European top cops who cut through red tape.[198]

Where terrorists could previously operate in one country and flee across the border to another when the police came too close, these sanctuaries in Western Europe have now become traps. Sanctuaries in Eastern Europe and across the Mediterranean are still viable, but more difficult to reach from many parts of Europe.

Latin America

While the American media were concentrating on the plight of the American hostages in Iran, 19 diplomats, including the American ambassador to Colombia, were being held hostage. This event underscores the importance of terrorism directed against American diplomats and business-men in Latin America.[199]

However, some Latin American countries have managed to eliminate terrorism, sometimes against great odds. One of the most efficient and deadly group of terrorists anywhere, the Tupamaros of Uruguay, came close to overwhelming the nation's democratic government. In 1977, the Uruguayan Parliament proclaimed a state of siege. Mass media were censored; the police were placed under military command; and an elite unit of 12,000 men was detailed exclusively to the task of routing the terrorists. Within several months, the Tupamaro organization was no longer a significant factor. Torture was used to induce prisoners to talk.[200] Similar tactics were used to decimate terrorist

---

[198]Brecher, p. 50.

[199]Everett G. Martin, "Latin America's Terrorist Network," Wall Street Journal, 15 April 1980, p. 25.

[200]Louis Heren, "Curbing Terrorism," Atlas World Press Review, January 1978, pp. 31-35.

organizations in Argentina and Brazil.[201]

Summary

This chapter reviewed the literature dealing with national responses to terrorism and with national response mechanisms. The greatest emphasis was on the situation in the United States under the four most recent administrations.

The American response to terrorism was revised as a result of the September, 1972, attack on Israeli athletes during the Munich Olympic Games. Immediately following the Olympic "massacre," President Nixon asked the secretary of state to chair a cabinet committee to consider the most effective means for preventing terrorism in the United States and abroad. The cabinet committee delegated its powers and responsibilities to a working group headed by the State Department representative and including all of the federal agencies having some interest in and responsibility for terrorist activities at home or abroad.

Under President Carter, this mechanism was greatly expanded. Instead of the two layers of control, one of which (the cabinet committee) rarely met, three were created. Primary responsibility for the management of terrorist incidents was vested in an appendage to the National Security Council. The Special Coordination Committee (SCC) of the NSC was chaired by the assistant to the president for national security affairs. This committee, which had a membership larger than the NSC itself, was responsible for crisis management, the resolution of jurisdictional disputes, coordination in the development of options, the implementation of presidential decisions, and the oversight of sensitive intelligence activities.

Reporting to the SCC was the Executive Committee on Terrorism (ECT), made up of representatives of the departments of State (chairman), Justice (deputy chairman), Defense, Treasury, Transportation, and Energy, the CIA, and the NSC staff. The ECT was responsible for handling matters of governmentwide policy formulation and operational coordination. Its primary concerns were with the response to major terrorism incidents and related issues, including the periodic testing of response capabilities. It was also responsible for long-term planning.

---

[201]Ibid.

The State Department's Working Group on Terrorism was given a greatly expanded membership and fewer responsibilities. In addition to State and Justice, members included the Agency for International Development, the Arms Control and Disarmament Agency, the Central Intelligence Agency, the Defense Intelligence Agency, the Department of the Army, the Department of Commerce, the Department of Energy, the Department of Transportation, the Department of the Treasury, the Federal Aviation Administration, the FBI, the Federal Preparedness Agency, the Immigration and Naturalization Service, the Center for Disease Control, the Joint Chiefs of Staff, the Law Enforcement Assistance Administration, the District of Columbia Police Department, the National Security Agency, the Nuclear Regulatory Commission, the Office of Management and Budget, the Office of the Secretary of Defense, the U.S. Coast Guard, the U.S. Customs Service, the U.S. mission to the United Nations, the U.S. Postal Service, the Secret Service, and the U.S. Marshal Service. This unwieldy group operated primarily through subcommittees, the most important of which was the Committee on Contingency Planning and Crisis Management.

The "lead agency" concept became institutionalized during the Carter administration. State and local governments are responsible for the management of terrorist incidents where no federal law has been broken. The Department of State is the lead agency for responding to international terrorist attacks that take place outside the territory of the United States. It also has a major interest in any terrorist action involving foreign diplomatic or other foreign official personnel. Terrorist incidents that involve the violation of federal law and which take place within the United States are usually managed by the Department of Justice, operating primarily through the FBI. The State Department is chiefly responsible for international cooperation in "legislating" against terrorism.

These elaborate coordinating mechanisms were largely ignored during the 444 days of the Iranian hostage crisis. Day-to-day developments were handled by the traditional State Department "desk" structure. Decisions were made by the president with the advice of the secretary of state, the national security adviser, and the secretary of defense. An informal "military committee" was formed by Brzezinski and included the secretary of defense, the chairman of the Joint Chiefs of Staff, and the director of the CIA.

The Reagan administration has made terrorism a major foreign and domestic policy issue. International terrorism is viewed as a Soviet tactic to gain important objectives. In terms of institutions, the measures taken to combat terrorism will be ordered by the president and his cabinet officers. The role of the NSC appears to have been greatly diminished from the days of Kissinger and Brzezinski.

Accurate and timely intelligence is a necessity if terrorism is to be curbed. In the United States, obtaining intelligence about terrorism is politically touchy, and disseminating it to the thousands of state and local units having a "need to know" is virtually impossible. Nixon ordered the CIA to engage in domestic espionage and operations against dissident groups and even established a special White House unit for the same purposes. The activities of the latter group resulted in the Watergate scandal and led to Nixon's forced resignation. Under Carter, the pendulum swung in the other direction: the CIA was limited to overseas operations, and strict guidelines were established to protect Americans against intelligence and operations excesses. President Reagan wants to unleash the CIA and other intelligence agencies and groups against domestic terrorists, but it remains to be seen whether he will succeed. Even if he does, the problem of how to inform the many state and local police departments of intelligence regarding known or suspected terrorists will remain.

The most basic decision concerning a national response to terrorism is whether to negotiate or to fight. Before the Munich "massacre," the United States pursued a flexible policy. After Munich, a no-ransom policy was adopted which, however, has been followed only sporadically. The policy was applied strictly in Khartoum, with the deaths of the American ambassador and his deputy chief of mission the result. The policy was not applied during the Iran crisis, where the United States followed a "carrot and stick" approach, also without significant success.

Those foreign nations which have been the most successful in curbing terrorism apply a flexible policy designed to save the lives of hostages as the first priority. The same policy is used by the New York City Police Department, which is generally considered to have an exemplary antiterrorist capability. Israel never negotiates, except to gain time as at Entebbe, and concentrates its efforts on making certain that the terrorists are killed, no matter what the cost to the hostages. Moreover, when a terrorist act takes place, it retaliates on the principle that several of its enemies must be killed for every Israeli who falls. However, this policy, in practice for nearly three decades, has not had the effect of eliminating terrorism. West Germany, which has enjoyed considerable success in coping with domestic terrorism, does negotiate.

A number of countries have managed to bring endemic terrorism under control. Turkey, which was almost prostrate, dealt terrorism a mortal blow when its generals assumed power and adopted a hard-line, impartial policy against terrorism from both the left and the right. In some parts of Latin America, the military has also been able to bring terrorism under control. These gains were, however, achieved at the cost of civil liberties.

West Germany has also managed to prevail over terrorism, but with a minimal effect on democratic liberties. The Germans gave their federal police force--roughly comparable to the FBI--the legal and material means to operate against terrorists in any jurisdiction in the nation. By this means, they eliminated one of the advantages terrorists enjoy in countries with a federal structure. They also computerized their records dealing with German and international terrorists. The West German computer bank is now regarded as Western Europe's primary defense against international terrorism. The Germans appear to have managed to obtain some of the advantages of a military dictatorship--centralized command and full coordination--without destroying their democratic political structure.

International efforts to combat terrorism have been ineffective except within limited areas and in questions of skyjacking. The world community cannot agree whether some groups are "terrorists" or "freedom fighters." World agreements are not likely until there is a solution to the Palestinian problem. On the other hand, the Western Europeans have had some success in dealing with terrorism through international cooperation. The United States concerts its antiterrorist actions with the West Europeans and with a number of other countries in North and South America.

CHAPTER 3

STUDY FINDINGS

This chapter analyzes and evaluates the information examined in preceding chapters. The purpose of the study is to review the existing response mechanisms of the United States and of those nations which have demonstrated an outstanding ability to cope effectively with terrorism, in order to develop an improved model for possible use by the United States. The elements entering into the development of a response mechanism include problems of definition, foreign and domestic policies, intelligence acquisition and dissemination, basic policies toward terrorism, efforts to secure international cooperation against terrorism, and the response structure itself.

Problems of Definition

The problems of defining terrorism were discussed in chapter 1. An inability of the international community to agree on a definition of terrorism has made it impossible for the United Nations to agree on measures to curb terrorism. Essentially, the inability to reach agreement is based on the adage that "one man's terrorist is another's freedom fighter." Presumably, the United States would not want Pakistan to apply sanctions against the Afghans fighting the Soviet Union and its indigenous political allies. The present prime minister of Israel was an avowed terrorist before the establishment of that country, but now inveighs against the "terrorist" Yasser Arafat who is trying to reverse the existing conditions. Problems of definition will almost certainly continue to complicate the search for international, universalist solutions.

Some limited gains have been achieved in circumscribed fields. There is now a workable body of international law dealing with skyjacking. In 1973, the United Nations General Assembly adopted the Convention on the Prevention and Punishment of Crimes Against Internationally Protected Persons, Including Diplomatic Agents, but this action has had little practical effect.

Definitional problems also have a direct impact on the federal response structure. Congress has at various times considered the possibility of making terrorism a federal crime. Legislation of this sort would have had the effect of bringing the FBI into each terrorist incident in the same way that it now takes the lead in kidnapping cases. Congressional efforts have consistently failed because of the inability to distinguish between terrorism and actions already considered criminal acts. Whether or not a specific criminal act is also a terrorist act depends on the motives of the perpetrators and on the political outlook of the individual or group making the judgment. Often, it is not possible to distinguish between a criminal and a terrorist act until the perpetrators have been apprehended and all the circumstances established in a court of law. By then, the response mechanism has already responded and the question has become academic.

The problem of definition has, therefore, thwarted attempts by the federal government to simplify the response structure by making terrorism a crime distinct from such crimes as espionage, sabotage, kidnapping, extortion, robbery, or taking hostages. Terrorists are guilty of all such acts, but so are criminals operating without political motives. Bombings are usually terrorist acts, but they may also be motivated by a simple desire for revenge. Because Congress cannot define terrorism in such a way as to satisfy legal tests of the definition, it cannot pass legislation making the FBI the lead agency in all domestic terrorist cases.

Foreign and Domestic Policies

Foreign and domestic national policies have a major impact on the incidence of terrorism. Domestically, the two major episodes of violence in recent American history were the race riots between 1965 and 1969 and the reaction against the Vietnam conflict from 1966 until the end of the American involvement in Indochina.

There was comparatively little that the United States government could do immediately to overcome the impact of long centuries of racism.[1] President Johnson had already pushed through Congress such important legislation as the Economic Opportunity Act of 1964, the Civil Rights Act of 1964, and the Voting Rights Act of 1965 before the cities erupted in racial violence. However, measures that could be taken--affirmative action programs and the appointment of study groups, for example--were instituted promptly. The problem was massive, societal in scope, and beyond the

---

[1]George M. Frederickson, White Supremacy: A Comparative Study in American and South African History (New York: Oxford University Press, 1981).

province of the federal government to solve alone, but for a time it was confronted head-on.

The government could have ended U.S. involvement in Vietnam with comparative ease, but it would not. The Vietnam conflict radicalized a large segment of the American people. Some of those radicalized turned to terrorism and were supported by enough sympathizers so that members of the Weather Underground, for instance, were able, for more than a decade, to live relatively normal lives without being detected.[2] The facts that the Vietnam conflict was never formally declared a war by Congress, that its prosecution was marked by flagrant government duplicity, that no vital American interests appeared to be involved, that it was fought by a conscript army drawn largely from the lower socioeconomic levels of American society, and that it appeared to be a continuation of the bankrupt colonial policies which the French government had had to abandon more than a decade earlier made the radicalization understandable. The response mechanism was the president himself; he may have been served poorly by some of his advisers, but he had chosen them and would brook no criticism from any of them on the question of whether the United States should be in Vietnam at all.

An example of the effect of domestic policies on terrorism is provided by the Basque problem in Spain and France. In France, where the Basques have always been free to cultivate their language and ethnic identity, Basque terrorism is not a problem. In Spain, where successive governments have attempted to integrate the Basques into a unified monarchy, a dictatorship, and a democratic monarchy, Basque terrorism poses a major threat to the government.

American foreign policies, depending on their nature, can lead to an outbreak of terrorism in other countries or can minimize its impact. What was perceived as President Reagan's nuclear saber-rattling resulted in a revival of Red Army terrorism in West Germany. His recent call for the removal of all nuclear weapons from both Western and Eastern Europe[3] may have the opposite effect. Were the United States to tilt toward the Palestinians and raise the hope that they can achieve their objectives without recourse to violence, the terrorism of the PLO fringe groups might well diminish or vanish entirely. The responsibility for pointing to the connection between violent opposition and the content of foreign policy belongs

---

[2]Lucinda Franks, "The Seeds of Terror," New York Times Magazine, 22 November 1981, pp. 34-59, 72-76.

[3]Peter McGrath, "Reagan's Peace Offensive," Newsweek, 30 November 1981, pp. 30-33.

to the Department of State (Office of Intelligence Research and Country Desks), the CIA, and the United States International Communication Agency.

Frequently, the United States can choose only the lesser of two evils in considering the connection between domestic and foreign policies and terrorism. When two NATO allies such as Greece and Turkey clash over Cyprus, the United States can incur the enmity of one (or even both) of the parties when it attempts to judge the case on its merits. A majority of the Puerto Rican people has voted on a number of occasions to retain its association with the United States. It would be difficult for the United States to accede to the violent demands of that minority of the Puerto Rican people seeking independence and engaging in terrorist acts to achieve it.

There are cases where a change of policy results in easing terrorist pressures. There are cases, as in Northern Ireland, where no viable political alternatives appear to exist; bowing to Provisional IRA pressures would almost certainly result in violence by the Protestants of Northern Ireland. There may also be cases, as when the Greeks attempted to seize Cyprus by force and were met by a superior Turkish counterforce, when to alter national policy in order to avoid terrorist actions could be considered cowardly and immoral.

Intelligence

Intelligence is basic in the struggle against terrorism. Sound and timely intelligence merits the use of the overworked word <u>essential</u>. Without good intelligence, the authorities are in the position of Plato's blind men feeling separate parts of an elephant and attempting to describe it; thus, the one who felt only the trunk thought he was handling a snake.

The first step in dealing with any hostage situation is to accumulate accurate intelligence, comparable in content to tactical intelligence in military operations. Organizations such as the New York City Police Department and the FBI are adept at discovering the salient facts about the locale and the perpetrators of an incident. The CIA was also successful in determining the location of the American hostages in Iran and the relevant conditions of their captivity.

What appears to be more difficult in the United States is accumulating and disseminating what might be called strategic intelligence. For the purposes of this study, "strategic intelligence" includes all types of

intelligence other than that needed to deal with an immediate terrorist situation. Intelligence of this kind
includes the names, characteristics, and membership of
terrorist or potentially terrorist organizations, the links
between various organizations, and their international
connections, if any. Methods of accumulating such intelligence data include observation, research, infiltration,
informants, mail interception, breaking and entering, and
electronic surveillance.

The United States has excellent capabilities for the
collection of strategic intelligence, particularly in the
realm of electronic surveillance. These capabilities seem
to be comparatively efficient and advanced in collecting
foreign intelligence (by the CIA, NSA, DIA, and State
Department). However, the major problem in acquiring
intelligence about domestic terrorism is the apparent
inability of the United States to do so effectively.

One major problem appears to be the absence of
coordination with respect to terrorism in the field of
domestic intelligence. One of the witnesses who appeared
before Congress stated that "there is no systematic approach
now extant in the Government for collection, storage,
retrieval, or analysis of relevant data about such crimes."[4]
In the foreign field, the CIA is responsible for the
coordination and dissemination of all intelligence reaching
the government. No comparable institution exists in the
domestic field, in part because the FBI has no jurisdiction
over state and local police forces. The latter are not
required, by law, to share their information with any
federal authority, and are often reluctant to do so for a
variety of reasons. Informing the FBI is time-consuming,
and small police departments probably do not have the
manpower or financial resources systematically to pass
information to the FBI or to the Secret Service. Equally
importantly, many local police departments are reluctant to
share their information with federal authorities because of
the Freedom of Information Act, which could make their
intelligence activities public knowledge.

There are also restrictions on the release of
information from the federal government to state and local
law enforcement agencies. Stored in the formidable CIA
computer is a very great quantity of information about
international terrorist groups which could be of interest to
local police authorities. There is now no mechanism in
operation to ensure that relevant intelligence available to
the CIA is channeled to state and local law enforcement
groups. On those occasions when the CIA tried to train

---

[4]David Hubbard, in _Terrorism, Part 1_, Hearings,
p. 2976.

local police forces in such areas as guerrilla tactics used by international terrorists, there was a public outcry against the attempt.

The most important problem, however, is the perceived conflict between civil liberties and the need for timely and accurate domestic intelligence about terrorism. Nixon "unleashed" the intelligence agencies against dissenters, even creating his own White House unit for the purpose, and the consequent abuses were so flagrant that Presidents Ford and Carter had to put the agencies back on the leash. President Reagan appears determined to put the CIA back in the domestic intelligence field and otherwise to emphasize the collection of intelligence against domestic terrorists. How far he intends to go and what the specific targets will be remain unclear. The Reagan administration has talked a great deal about "terrorism" but has not yet tried to define it.

Because individuals and groups merely interested in expressing their right to dissent have suffered intrusions on their privacy and even harassment in the past does not mean that the same abuses will take place in the future. However, the great abuses of the intelligence function during Nixon's presidency will make it more difficult to develop a properly controlled preventive or strategic intelligence-gathering capacity.

The difficulty comes in determining what would constitute "proper" controls. Choosing individuals of great probity to head those government departments and agencies concerned with domestic intelligence is not enough. Successive directors of the FBI have engaged in suspect activities and one former head of the Justice Department has subsequently served time in prison. The concept of congressional supervision is one solution. However, Congress is a leaky sieve when it comes to safeguarding secrets, and some congressional committees become coopted by the federal services they attempt to oversee. The appointment of special prosecutors independent both of the executive branch and of Congress when allegations of abuses surface may prove to be one solution. Another might be the appointment of independent ombudsmen in those government agencies dealing with domestic intelligence agencies. The integrity of the Government Accounting Office is widely respected; using it or a similar office to cope with the problem might be a profitable avenue to explore. Students of the subject of terrorism who believe that a greater domestic intelligence effort is required have generally not addressed themselves to the problem of avoiding the abuses of the past.

The Policy of No Concessions

Since the September, 1972, terrorist attack on Israeli athletes at the Munich Olympics, the United States has had a formal policy of not negotiating with terrorists. The policy has been honored as much in its breach as in its observance, and has come under criticism from a number of sources.

In general, when the no-concessions policy has been applied strictly, the hostages taken have been killed. This was the case with Dan Mitrione in Uruguay and Ambassador Noel in the Sudan. Where the United States and/or the host government negotiated, the hostages taken have been freed. Such cases include Ambassador Clinton Knox in Haiti, Ambassador C. Burke Elbrick in Brazil, and Terrance Leonhardy in Mexico. Hostages have been released even when the host government has met only a part of the terrorists' demands. On a number of occasions, demands have been met, hostages have been freed, and the terrorists have then been apprehended and punished.

In practice, the no-concessions policy applies only to United States official personnel working overseas. They are among the prime targets of international terrorists. The other major targets, American businessmen overseas, work for companies that do not feel they can hope to attract capable employees if they adopt a policy similar to that of the American government. Invariably, the concerned corporations negotiate and make every effort to have their employees released, sometimes spending very large sums of money in the process.

The no-concessions policy is supposed to apply to all terrorist incidents, but has rarely been applied inside the United States. When the Hanafi Muslims seized the Islamic Center (the Washington mosque) and the B'nai B'rith building in Washington, D.C., the hostages taken were released following negotiations between the hostage takers and three Muslim ambassadors stationed in Washington. The basic policy of the New York City Police Department is always to contain the incident and then negotiate.

The no-concessions policy was endorsed by the Carter administration but ignored when the American embassy in Teheran was seized by a group of Iranian militants on November 4, 1979. During the 444 days of the Americans' captivity, the United States government negotiated frenetically with a number of Iranian politicians through a number of foreign intermediaries. At the end, the Iranians received their frozen assets back and the United States saw its hostages return home. However, the Iranians presumably used the hostages for their own political purposes for well over a year, releasing them only when they had become a political liability for the Khomeini regime.

The difference between the Ford and Carter reactions to the taking of hostages reflects a continuing dilemma for the United States in enunciating and implementing a coherent policy regarding how to deal with hostage situations. In the Mayaguez incident, President Ford expended 38 military lives in order to release the 39 seamen of the Mayaguez. His successor declared openly that he was putting the lives of the hostages in Iran first and negotiated, but then attempted a military rescue which, had it succeeded, would almost certainly have resulted in the deaths of some of the hostages and military personnel involved.

To be credible, a policy toward terrorism needs to be applied consistently and to be perceived by all as being backed by effective means. The United States has never applied a tough policy consistently. Potential terrorists know what to expect from the Israelis, but no such certainty exists insofar as the American response is concerned. The United States probably does not now have the means needed to repeat the Mayaguez rescue almost anywhere in the world. It has the power to destroy completely almost any country in the world, but does not seem to have the means to carry out Entebbe-type operations effectively.

Inconsistent application of the no-concessions policy appears to be implicit in the very nature of the American political system. Most democratic countries have a parliamentary form of government in which the prime minister emerges from and is dependent on the parliament. The last two American presidents have come from outside the political establishment. Indeed, they campaigned against the Washington establishment in order to gain power. Once elected, they were bound to try to do things differently than had their predecessors.

The personal imprint a U.S. president places on the government bureaucracy is greater than that possible in a parliamentary form of government. Nixon sought to treat dissenters as terrorists, ruining himself in the process, but achieved little of note in the struggle against national and international terrorism. Ford tended to speak softly but carry a big stick, as the Mayaguez incident illustrated. Carter emphasized human rights, continued Ford's emphasis on due process in domestic intelligence matters, and destroyed his chances for reelection when his policies respecting the Iranian hostage crisis were viewed as weak and vacillating. Reagan began his administration by linking international terrorism with the Soviet Union but has thus far done little to strike back at either. The Reagan administration has issued thinly veiled threats against Libya, Cuba, and Guatemala, but nothing tangible has resulted. Such swings of the pendulum are less likely in most democracies with a parliamentary form of government.

The theory behind the no-concessions policy--that terrorism must not result in tangible gains for the terrorists--has been disputed by a number of students of the subject. One alternative is a flexible policy in which negotiation with the terrorists always takes place. Negotiations may constitute mere delaying tactics, or an attempt may be made to scale down the terrorists' demands. Options are kept open. Still another policy would be to place humanitarian considerations first. Under such a policy, every effort would be made to free the hostages. Wherever possible, terrorists would be captured rather than killed. The objectives of a "humanitarian" policy are to enable the government to capture the high moral ground, to undercut the terrorists' claims that the government is inhumane, and to give mental health professionals an opportunity to study and possibly to rehabilitate the terrorists.

As indicated earlier, the no-concessions policy is hardest on American official personnel overseas. A statistical case could be made demonstrating that it is now more dangerous to be in the Foreign Service than to be in the American military forces. Private Americans overseas are not bound by the government's policy, and their companies usually negotiate and pay ransom. In defense of the no-concessions policy, it is often argued that American diplomats are soldiers in the Cold War and must take their chances.

The fallacy in the "cold-war soldier" argument is that official personnel overseas are not trained and equipped to serve in combat. A commander who sent an unarmed, untrained patrol out to reconnoiter a territory known to be dangerous should and probably would be court-martialed. If the analogy is apt, all American official personnel sent overseas should take courses in combat shooting in addition to their usual classes at the Foreign Service Institute. They should be provided with arms and equipment capable of dealing with the threats likely to be encountered. Instead of cost-of-living and hardship allowances, personnel in high-risk areas should receive combat pay. Personnel sent overseas should be told clearly that they will be regarded as soldiers in the Cold War and will, therefore, be treated as expendable by their government. Security at diplomatic and consular missions overseas should be strengthened accordingly, with American personnel living in militarily secure compounds. Personnel sent overseas should be of military age and preferably single.

Diplomatic and consular missions of the new "military" type would, however, be virtually useless as representational and reporting posts. Foreign service personnel are expected to circulate within the country to which they are assigned, to make friends for themselves and the United States, to learn as much as possible from a wide

range of individuals, and to report the situation in the
country accurately. These objectives cannot be carried out
by Foreign Service personnel living in fortified compounds
which they are afraid to leave.

There is no logical reason to assume that a clearly
stated but sporadically observed policy is any better than
an ambiguous or flexible one. How to deal with terrorism is
one area in which actions speak louder than words. Where
the circumstances are such that the United States can
conduct an Entebbe- or Mayaguez-type operation with a good
chance of success, the president could authorize it. Where
the circumstances make it clear that military action could
result in loss of the hostages, the United States would
negotiate. In most cases, the primary consideration would
be the safe return of the hostages, but there could be
departures from this principle if the probable cost to the
nation would be too great.

The adoption of a flexible policy to replace the
present stance of no concessions could be justified on the
basis of national self-interest. The United States is under
no obligation to inform its enemies in advance of the course
it intends to follow when hostile acts are committed.
Enunciation of tough policies that cannot be implemented in
practice smacks of mere bravado. The range of policies that
can be followed under the umbrella of ambiguity is large
enough to encompass both humanitarian concern and the
Israeli "eye-for-an-eye" approach. What is important is to
develop a policy that can be applied in whatever way best
serves the interests of the United States.

The responsibility for developing and proposing to
the president any new policy for dealing with terrorism
should probably be one of the first tasks undertaken by any
new response mechanism established by the federal government. The arguments for and against the existing policy
have been presented in some detail in the pertinent literature.

International Cooperation Against Terrorism

Political realities and the difficulties involved in
defining terrorism limit the extent to which international
action against terrorism can be orchestrated through the
United Nations. The impasse in the UN does not mean,
however, that international cooperation against terrorism is
doomed to fail.

United Nations resolutions have been adopted with
respect to air piracy and sabotage, and attacks against
diplomatic and other internationally protected personnel. A

growing number of nations has acceded to conventions concerning these questions. United Nations members condemned the seizure and holding of the American hostages in Iran. It is quite possible that other aspects of terrorism will become so repugnant to the world community that additional measures can be taken through the UN.

In order for additional actions against terrorism to materialize, someone will have to take the initiative. The question has to be inscribed on the UN General Assembly agenda; an international lobbying effort through American diplomatic posts must be undertaken; and internal position papers need to be written. For the initiative to have any chance of success, an accurate reading of the international climate must be made by American diplomatic posts. It is not clear whether any organization or group inside the United States government would now have the responsibility for following and pushing such UN action. The Bureau of International Organization Affairs handles UN affairs within the State Department, but it includes no one who follows terrorism in particular. The Working Group on Terrorism is not UN-oriented. It is quite possible, therefore, that opportunities to obtain United Nations agreements will not be fully exploited.

Cooperation between the United States and its allies can be useful. The decision concerning hijacking at the Bonn Summit in July, 1978, is an example. The eight countries represented at that summit agreed to suspend immediately their commercial air services to all countries refusing to prosecute or extradite aircraft hijackers or to return hijacked aircraft. Those eight nations are responsible for most of the world's commercial air traffic, so the declaration has substance. Other measures, including suspension of financial aid, trade, and diplomatic contacts, might well be considered by the same governments. It is also possible that additional governments might be induced to adhere to the existing limited agreement.

International cooperation is also important in the field of intelligence. The Reagan administration has apparently emphasized this aspect of the antiterrorist campaign. Some information comes through the medium of Interpol. The remainder is probably channeled to the CIA from its counterparts in friendly foreign countries. Once the information has been acquired, the problem becomes one of internal coordination: the relevant information must be provided to the FBI or to state and local police forces.

The problem of internal coordination of internationally developed intelligence cannot easily be resolved. Even when information is divulged on the usual need-to-know basis, the smaller police departments would have problems dealing with the quantities of material made available.

There would be problems of security clearances for all those receiving the information and of protecting the materials once they are transmitted to the local level of law enforcement.

Coordination between the CIA and the FBI has, historically, been less than perfect. The CIA may, for example, wish to protect a sensitive source and therefore not inform the FBI of some terrorist in the United States. Apprehending the terrorist or keeping him under surveillance might be of considerable importance, but protecting a valuable asset overseas might be even more important to the CIA's hierarchy. Consequently, it cannot be assumed that all of the relevant intelligence collected through international sources will be made available even to the FBI, much less to state and local police departments.

Cooperation among selected countries could also be envisaged in the areas of black propaganda, disinformation, and bogus organizations. "Black" propaganda--propaganda materials purporting to emanate from some unofficial source--could be used to create confusion in the ranks of international terrorism. Disinformation--the systematic funneling of false information--could be used for the same purpose. An organization funded by Western governments might recruit terrorists and use them in operations serving the interests of the participating governments.

Optimum use of the United Nations, foreign-developed intelligence, and opportunities for various operations against international terrorism depend on the existence of an appropriate response mechanism in the United States. That response mechanism is deficient in a number of important respects.

The American Response Structure

The United States response structure has a number of undesirable characteristics. Balkanization (administrative fragmentation) is probably its most prominent deficiency, but there are others.

Instability

The response structure has suffered from a lack of continuity and stability. Nixon took the lead in developing an American response structure as a result of the shock felt around the world over the attack on the Israeli athletes at the Munich Olympics. Ford made no significant changes in the structure except in the field of domestic intelligence gathering. Carter developed an elaborate bureaucracy despite his pledge to streamline government operations.

Reagan has not settled on a definitive structure, but appears to have simplified considerably the one inherited from the Carter administration.

The structure has suffered from frequent changes in personnel. Personnel instability will continue as long as important parts of the structure are staffed by Foreign Service officers. It is State Department policy not to keep such officers in the same Washington job for more than two years. Officers themselves generally want to go overseas, where the pay and perquisites are better and where careers are made. Within the Department of State itself, most jobs outside the geographical bureaus are regarded as inferior assignments. What is required is the assignment of individuals willing to make a career of the study of terrorism. Such individuals are more likely to be found in the CIA, the Justice Department, and any other agency not dominated by the Foreign Service.

Distance Between the Expert and the Decision Maker

The distance between the most knowledgeable personnel and those who make decisions is one of the most serious criticisms that can be leveled against the American way of conducting such activities as the war against terrorism. The federal government's methods of operation are the antithesis of those used by the New York City Police Department, where the borough commander is deliberately placed in charge of implementing policy in any terrorist incident. The individual in charge is not the mayor, not the police commissioner, and not the FBI agent-in-charge, but the police officer who knows the area best and who will ultimately have to live in it with the consequences of his actions.

On the federal level, decisions are usually made by the president or by his close associates in the cabinet or the National Security Council. The decision-making levels of the departments of State and Justice are staffed by political appointees who must invariably spread themselves thin, since all important problems of whatever nature come to their desks. In an international terrorist crisis, an expert--a country director or desk officer who will probably have spent at least six years working in or on a particular country--will brief an assistant secretary of state for the region, who will brief the undersecretary or a similar official, who will brief the secretary, who will then brief the president. In the step-by-step ascent through the bureaucracy toward the president, a great deal of expert knowledge and "feel" for the problem becomes dissipated or altered. When the president makes his decision, it is on the basis of a short "action" memorandum, supplemented by a short briefing by the secretary of state. Very often, action memoranda are prepared not by the State Department experts but by a member of the NSC staff who follows a large number of different countries and problems.

The hemorrhaging of understanding and expert knowledge is even greater when the working level wishes to undertake some action in the absence of an immediate crisis or a specific mandate from the White House. The Iranian experts in the State Department who attempted counseling President Carter to follow a different course of action were never able to reach him. In order for a working-level suggestion to reach the decision-making level, it must receive so many lateral and vertical clearances that the crisis may be over or the opportunity lost by the time the suggestion arrives--if it arrives at all.[5]

It is outside the scope of this study to suggest ways in which better use can be made of the expert knowledge found in the federal government. Insofar as terrorism is concerned, the only structure that would seem able to marry expertise and decision making is one that is organization-ally close to the president. The NSC and the Office of Management and Budget (OMB) derive their power from their proximity to the president. President Carter was the only recent chief executive to develop part of such a structure--the Special Coordination Committee (SCC) of the National Security Council, to handle terrorism and other matters. The SCC was close enough to the president to have instant access to him through Brzezinski and administra-tively important enough to be able to tap all the resources of the federal government. However, the SCC was a cabinet-level group that did not have experts on terrorism on its own staff.

The Federal Emergency Management Agency, which Carter created, did not solve the problem of bringing together experts and decision makers. It could have brought together a group of experts on contingency planning for terrorist attacks. However, the agency is outside the Executive Office of the President: just another agency among many. Moreover, it has nothing to do with the management of terrorist crises, merely with their aftermaths.

Distance Between Experts

Another major defect in the existing response mecha-nism is the distance between individual experts scattered

---

[5]Administrations vary in the degree to which they bureaucratize the decision-making process. President Kennedy, who was very much interested in foreign affairs, dealt directly with the working level of the State Department and the CIA, but he was an exception to the general rule.

through the federal bureaucracy. These experts are in the departments of Justice and State, the FBI, the intelligence community, the FAA, some 20 other agencies, and private research organizations.

Many of the experts can be brought together as needed in a crisis. In the absence of a crisis, however, each goes his own way, concentrating on his own part of the overall problem. There is no cross-fertilization of ideas such as would result from working together on a regular basis. Moreover, some of the individuals whose advice would be sought in a crisis pay only sporadic attention to the problem of terrorism. One agency or group may make danger- ously inaccurate assumptions about the doctrines, practices, and capabilities of other departments and agencies with responsibilities in the struggle against terrorism.

Furthermore, lacking is the expansion of knowledge that comes from having a "critical mass" of experts working together on a common problem. The physical sciences would have fewer achievements to their credit if there were not a constant exchange of information and a cross-fertilization of ideas. In the field of terrorism, there is no mechanism for ensuring the constant exchange of information and ideas. Unclassified periodicals help, but they are not an accept- able substitute for bringing the experts from various organizations together either on a permanent basis--in one agency--or frequently on a regular basis.

Balkanization

Responsibility for the management of terrorist attacks is so divided among federal agencies and state and local officials that it is frequently difficult to know who is in charge. In a typical domestic case, in James Kelly's words: "We have a State police captain, a local police chief, an FBI agent, then we have a postal inspector because the threat came through the mail--and it all started over here where the sheriff had the original jurisdiction."[6]

The confusion that existed during the seizure by a group of Hanafi Muslims of the Islamic Center and the B'nai B'rith building in Washington, D.C., in January, 1977, shows that the hypothetical case cited by Kelly is not an exag- geration. There were major differences of opinion between the District of Columbia police, the FBI, and the Secret Service regarding how to handle the incident. At one point in the crisis, the District of Columbia police decided to assault the B'nai B'rith building from the roof, but were unable to do so when it was discovered that they had no

---

[6]James Kelly, in Terrorism, Part 1, Hearings, p. 3074.

personnel able to rappel out of a helicopter. "The chaos was frightening," one participant recalled later. If it had not been for the intervention of the three Muslim ambassadors, the Hanafi Muslims "would have been chucking bodies out the windows."[7]

The situation in terms of the command structure becomes even more complex when a terrorist incident has international ramifications. When Croatian extremists took over a TWA plane in September, 1976, one government official involved in the incident later declared that responsibility for management "bounced around the Government like a floating crap game."[8] The FAA claimed jurisdiction. Because the American airliner had been hijacked in the United States, the FBI believed that it had the primary responsibility. As soon as the airliner crossed into Canadian airspace before going to France, the State Department became involved. As soon as the plane arrived in France, the French shot out its tires and indicated a refusal to negotiate, even though all of the hijackers' demands had already been met.

The Croatian hijacking incident has been described in sufficient detail so that it can be taken as a case study of how the "lead agency" principle works in practice. As soon as the incident was reported, L. Douglas Heck, coordinator of the Cabinet Committee to Combat Terrorism, went to his office in the FAA building in Washington. He was joined there by the transportation secretary and the chief of the FAA, intelligence and logistical experts from the State Department, FAA technical experts, FAA medical advisers, and FAA and State Department psychiatrists. This task force was patched to the NSC by phone. Task forces were also established by the State Department and the Department of Justice. The transportation secretary and the chief of the FAA were both senior to Heck, and he could, of course, be overruled by the NSC.

Meanwhile, at the scene, the New York City police and the FBI were jointly in charge of handling the incident while the plane remained on the ground. The FAA did not become officially involved until the plane took off, and remained in charge only as long as the aircraft was in American airspace.

A large number of federal agencies have some interest in terrorism. The State Department's Working Group

---

[7]Gregory F. Rose, "The Terrorists Are Coming," Politics Today, July/August 1978, p. 52.

[8]Brian M. Jenkins, in An Act to Combat Terrorism, Hearings, p. 108.

on Terrorism under Carter included State (chairman), Justice (deputy chairman), the Agency for International Development, the Arms Control and Disarmament Agency, the Central Intelligence Agency, the Defense Intelligence Agency, the Department of the Army, the Department of Commerce, the Department of Energy, the Department of Transportation, the Department of the Treasury, the Federal Aviation Administration, the Federal Bureau of Investigation, the Federal Preparedness Agency, the Immigration and Naturalization Service, the Center for Disease Control, the Joint Chiefs of Staff, the Law Enforcement Assistance Administration, the District of Columbia Police Department, the National Security Agency, the Nuclear Regulatory Commission, the Office of Management and Budget, the Office of the Secretary of Defense, the United States Coast Guard, the United States Customs Service, the United States mission to the UN, the United States Postal Service, the Secret Service, and the United States Marshal Service. Merely convening a group including representatives of all of these bodies must have been difficult and time-consuming.

At the same time, there must certainly be occasions which require the expertise of some group representative with respect to somewhat out-of-the-mainstream antiterrorism operations. For example, in the recent case of the alleged Libyan terrorists dispatched into the United States from Canada or from Mexico to assassinate the highest leaders of the United States government,[9] the special knowledge of the INS and of the Customs Service would have been invaluable. Inputs from the State Department, the CIA, the FBI, the Defense Intelligence Agency (DIA), the NSA, and the Secret Service would also have been required.

A distinction, based on communications capabilities, between agencies should be made in order to refine the analysis. Agencies with worldwide communications capabilities include the State Department, the CIA, and the DIA. The CIA and the DIA generally use State Department communications facilities and are not as readily accessible to large numbers of representatives from other agencies as is the State Department. The DIA does not have available on the spot the large numbers of experts on virtually all of the world's areas and problems that the State Department and the CIA have. The State Department can communicate in minutes with any of its embassies by using a precedence indicator ensuring that a particular telegram is encrypted and dispatched ahead of all others.

[9]"The Kaddafi Hit Squad at Large?" Newsweek, 14 December 1981, pp. 36-37; David M. Alpern, "Coping with a Plot to Kill the President," Newsweek, 21 December 1981, pp. 16-17, 19.

The State Department also has a special secure area to handle the operations of special working groups. The operations center is staffed 24 hours a day by Foreign Service officers as well as fairly senior representatives of the military services. Priority telegrams are received immediately by personnel in the operations center. It also has such additional sources of information as news-ticker machines. Important telegrams are repeated automatically to the NSC. There are secure facilities for telephoning the White House, military bases, and some embassies. In periods of major crisis, the geographical bureaus staff the center continuously with key personnel. There are sleeping quarters and other amenities for those officers required to work at odd hours and around the clock.

It was therefore a natural step to house the Working Group on Terrorism (WGT) in the Department of State. In any international terrorist crisis, the needed personnel, communications, and other facilities are already available. All that was required was to add personnel from other agencies that might have a special interest or expertise in the given incident.

In the case of the Libyan assassins allegedly infiltrated into the United States,[10] the Immigration and Naturalization Service, the Customs Service, and the Secret Service would have an invaluable role to play in analyzing developments and planning countermeasures. These organizations, however, do not have the communications capabilities nor the ready access to information and policy makers that the State Department does. It therefore appears logical to have the WGT housed in the State Department whenever there is an international aspect to a terrorist incident.

The advantages enjoyed by the State Department in cases of international terrorism do not apply to purely domestic cases of terrorism. In the latter, the Department of Justice would appear to have the files, personnel, and communications needed to deal most effectively with the problem. The State Department has a number of attorneys on its staff, but they all concentrate on problems of international law or of domestic law involving foreign countries. They do not have the background or information needed to provide useful information concerning purely domestic terrorism. There is, therefore, little reason to handle domestic cases of terrorism out of the State Department.

---

[10]"Libyan Assassins Now After Reagan?" U.S. News & World Report, 14 December 1981, p. 5; "Why Reagan Moved Against Libya's Qadhafi," "A President Under Wraps," and "A Broker in Global Terror," U.S. News & World Report, 21 December 1981, pp. 10-11.

Insofar as there is a federal interest in a domestic act of terrorism, it is logical to handle it from the Justice Department, which has the ties to the FBI, the files, and the informed personnel that the State Department does not.

There consequently appears to be a clear distinction between the response mechanism needs posed by a domestic terrorist incident and one with international implications.

In such units of the federal government as State, Justice, the CIA, and the DIA, it is possible to create staffs of individuals spending most of their time working on terrorism. In such smaller units as the AID, the ACDA, the INS, the Coast Guard, and the OMB, it is unlikely that even one individual can be allowed the "luxury" of working exclusively on terrorism. Therefore, in order to enable all of the parts of a task force to work together harmoniously and effectively, it has been perceived as necessary to have them work together on a regular, continuing basis. If real-world crises do not develop on such a basis, hypothetical crises must be used for practice purposes.

In the American system of government, the most important member of any crisis task force is the president. Even where he does not play an active role, there is always the possibility that he will say or do something to alter the situation dramatically. As case in point is the Khartoum incident, where the efforts of the working group to negotiate the release of Ambassador Noel and his deputy chief of mission were undercut by the statement of President Nixon that the United States would not negotiate. The two American diplomats were thereupon killed by their terrorist captors. The impending negotiations might have failed and the hostages might have been killed anyway, but the Nixon statement guaranteed their immediate execution. It is, accordingly, of the uppermost importance that the president and the members of his immediate staff be aware of and sympathetic to the efforts that the working level is making. Coordination between working-level agencies is always important; their coordination with the White House in invariably crucial.

A number of suggestions have been made in the literature to improve the response mechanism of the United States. Most of these suggested improvements relate to domestic terrorism.

A number of witnesses before congressional committees advanced the idea of creating special teams to assist state and local law enforcement officials. The teams would be positioned in various regions of the country and would include specialists in such disciplines as criminology, psychiatry, media analysis, sociology, linguistics, and cultural anthropology. There would be a permanent staff on the federal level in order to establish, control, and coordinate the regional teams, which would be dispatched to the spot whenever there was an incident of domestic terrorism with which local officials could not cope. The teams would meet frequently enough in Washington or in their particular regions to ensure that they were fully briefed on trends and countermeasures. Members of the teams would have security clearances of the sort permitting them to read all relevant materials.

One witness believed that such teams should be established in each state and in most major cities. If so, there would have to be a larger federal role in the form of a permanent corps of terrorism experts who could be flown at short notice to the site of a terrorist attack to concert with the local team, assisting local law enforcement officials.

The fact that teams of the kind recommended have not been established suggests that the concept may have some drawbacks. In the first place, it would be difficult to find people of the requisite stature in their respective fields both able and willing to devote the necessary time to the enterprise. The better the qualifications of prospective team members, the less likely they are to have the time to devote to an ongoing program. Secondly, the greater the prestige of the team members, the more likely they are to want to have their views on tactics prevail, with possibly undesirable consequences for the management of terrorist incidents.

The talent probably could be found to establish several regional teams, but it is doubtful that personnel of the caliber required could be found for terrorism teams in every state and major city. Even if the personnel could be found, the fiscal restraints currently imposed by the Reagan administration would seem to preclude such an ambitious program.

Problems of coordination among federal agencies and between federal agencies and state and local groups are not limited to the field of terrorism. In an effort to fight organized crime, the federal government has been spending about $100 million a year without achieving much success. Few organized crime figures spend much time in jail as a result of the federal strike forces attacking organized crime. Moreover, there is little coordination among the various federal law enforcement agencies assigned to the task forces.[11] A major gap in the existing response

---

[11]Mary Thornton, "GAO Criticizes Strike Force on Organized Crime," Washington Post, 7 December 1981, pp. A-1, A-5.

structure is the comparative lack of attention paid to media questions. Capturing the attention of the world for a cause through the mass media is commonplace. The CIA has stated that terrorists anxious to gain maximum publicity are almost certain to be able to achieve that goal. It is generally agreed in the literature that whatever can be done to curb the media's appetite for the sensational would be a help in stemming the terrorist tide. Under the American system, the only way this objective can be achieved is through education and cooperation. If enough scholars point the finger at the media as part of the terrorist problem and if the public reacts negatively to the extensive coverage given every terrorist action, the media might find it in their interest to cover this aspect of the news in a more restrained fashion. In any event, media specialists and psychological warfare experts need to play a larger role than they have heretofore in the federal control structure.

Response Structures of Other Nations

The experience of other nations with terrorism is, perhaps unexpectedly, of only limited value to the United States. In most cases, the political systems, nature of the threats, and external circumstances of other countries are so different that American applications of foreign tactics and strategies would be irrelevant or even impossible.

Terrorism can, assuredly, be brought under control even where it has been endemic for years. The Turks and some Latin American nations have almost destroyed strong terrorist movements by imposing military rule. The price for freedom from endemic and widespread terrorism has been the loss by the public of civil and political liberties.

The nature of the existing terrorist threat in the United States does not justify such a response to it--one which would probably polarize the nation, merely exacerbating the situation. In view of the Kent State incident, it seems likely that use of the military in putting down any terrorists short of revolutionaries attempting to overthrow the government should be under strict civilian control.

An example of using the military in a democratic society is the British experience in Ulster (Northern Ireland). Military involvement, however, has been limited to Northern Ireland, and the principle of civilian ascendancy has not been violated. Every attempt has been made to reach a political settlement. Furthermore, Great Britain has tried to reduce its purely military presence in Northern Ireland by turning security responsibilities over to indigenous forces.

Although Israel is frequently cited as a model of efficiency in dealing with terrorism, it has little to teach the United States. Israel is at war with all of its Arab neighbors except Egypt. Palestinian terrorism against Israeli targets is merely a continuation of genuine war with limited means. Israel feels justified, because of the past and present history of the Jewish people and the enmity of most of its neighbors, in adopting a harsh policy of reprisals. The United States is not in the same situation, either with respect to its neighbors or to a threat against its political sovereignty and integrity. Moreover, the evidence suggests that Israeli policy, far from preventing terrorism, tends to escalate the violence in the region until full-blown war periodically results. Yet again, the Israeli response mechanism, marked by strict cabinet control over antiterrorist operations, is more suitable for a very small country than for the large and complex American federal structure.

One element of the Israeli experience that could be adopted by the United States is the policy of reprisals against countries harboring and sponsoring terrorist activities. Reports that Libya has sent assassination teams into the United States have led to administration promises that retribution would be swift and certain.[12] There have been threats against Cuba as well, but the United States has proved singularly inept in exacting retribution from that country.

The two nations whose experiences with terrorism seem most pertinent to the United States are West Germany and Canada. Both have democratic, federal forms of government and respect civil liberties.

The Germans were able to cope with their domestic terrorism by strengthening the role and capabilities of their FBI, the Bundeskriminalamt. The German Parliament provided this body with jurisdiction over most terrorist incidents. In the few excluded types of cases, the federal police force could be requested to intervene by the state authorities or ordered into action by the federal government. In addition, the federal police force was made responsible for maintaining and disseminating centralized information about terrorism and related activities. The Bundeskriminalamt responded by developing the most complete computer data base concerning terrorism available in the Western world, with the possible exception of the CIA. West

---

[12]James Kelly, Douglas Brew, and Adam Zagorin, "Searching for Hit Teams," *Time*, 21 December 1981, pp. 16-20, 22; George J. Church, Laurence I. Barrett, and Frank Melville, "Some Sanctions That May Not Work," *Time*, 21 December 1981, pp. 24-26.

Germany has been able to cope with its own terrorists and to assist other Western European countries in their struggle against terrorism.

For the United States to emulate the West Germans would require some significant legislation. Congress would have to make certain categories of crimes a federal responsibility. The Germans turned over to their federal police responsibility for such matters as internationally organized, illicit traffic in weapons, ammunition, explosives, drugs, and false currency, crimes committed against certain high officers of the government and its guests, and all cases involving the diplomatic corps. The approach represented by enumerating specific crimes seems easier to implement than one requiring a definition of "terrorism."

Duplicating the West German computer capability would be much more difficult in the United States. Such disparate groups as civil libertarians and pro-gun associations would be extremely reluctant to have the government collect and computerize the records on all Americans necessary to make the system a success. Only the Internal Revenue Service and the Social Security System now have comprehensive files on virtually all Americans, and these files can only be used for fiscal purposes defined by law. Previous attempts to use information already in the government's hands to accomplish such objectives as tracking down illegal aliens have been strenuously and successfully resisted.

In order to copy the West German system successfully, something in the nature of national identity cards would have to be accepted by the American people. The United States is one of the few technologically advanced nations without such cards. It is also one of the very few nations which does not know how many of its residents, and which ones, are in the country illegally. This ignorance makes it difficult to identify and thwart potential terrorists.

The American social-science establishment could profit from one aspect of the German experience. German social scientists studied terrorism in its social context rather than concentrating on the aberrant individual. Theories of individual deviance were discarded after psychiatric examination of members of the Baader-Meinhof Gang revealed no symptoms of neurosis or psychosis. By contrast, American scholarship has sought to delineate a terrorist-prone type or has compiled general statistics which are significantly suspect because of definitional problems.

Canada, which also has a federal structure, was able to cope with the violence of the Quebec separatists only by

invoking the War Measures Act for the first time in peace-
time. Under the provisions of this act, the federal cabinet
was provided with unrestricted authority to issue orders and
regulations dealing with the emergency. The suspension of
constitutional guarantees, for instance, was permissible.
The government was able to cut through jurisdictional lines
with the stroke of a pen.

Making the Canadian government's task simpler were
the excesses of the Quebec terrorists, including the
kidnapping and murder of Minister Pierre Laporte. The
popular revulsion that this and similar actions inspired
rendered more palatable the Draconian measures undertaken by
the government. Hundreds of members of the Quebec Liberation Front were arrested without due process, enabling
authorities to find the individuals responsible for the
Laporte murder.

Many Canadians regret that their government has no
middle ground between the War Measures Act and normal application of the country's criminal code provisions. Application of the act was, perhaps, justified by the threat to
Canada's territorial integrity, but the emergency was not
quite as dire as a wartime situation.

It is difficult to see how the Canadian experience
can serve as any sort of model for the United States.
Constitutional guarantees were curtailed for Japanese-
Americans during World War II, but the incarceration of the
Nisei was illegal, a fact overlooked in the hatred and panic
following the Japanese attack on Pearl Harbor. Even a
congressional declaration of war would not have the same
effects as invocation of the War Measures Act did in Canada.
In any event, against what groups or what country would war
be declared? A decade and a half ago when black activists
were systematically setting fire to parts of major cities,
no thought was given to placing the country on a war footing
in the legal sense. Curfews were instituted in specific
cities during the height of the rioting and looting, but
that was all.

The situation of the United States is unique. No
other nation has the same political system and social
climate. It is instructive to review the experience of
foreign countries in dealing with terrorism, but it is not
possible to adopt their remedies without substantial
modifications. The United States has to develop its own
improved policies and mechanisms, based on its own needs and
traditions.

CHAPTER 4

THE MODEL U.S. RESPONSE STRUCTURE

The existing United States response mechanism for
dealing with terrorism is generally regarded by experts in
the field as inadequate. It has been marked by instability
in institutions and personnel. There is a lack of communication between the experts and the decision makers and
between experts in the various agencies concerned with
terrorism. Responsibility for the management of terrorist
incidents is so divided among federal agencies and state and
local governments that it is frequently difficult to know
who is in charge. Responsibility can shift rapidly from one
agency to another during the course of a single terrorist
incident, so that its management is almost certainly bound
to suffer.

This chapter sets forth what is considered an
improved model for the American response structure in
dealing with both domestic and international terrorism. The
following analysis is based on the materials developed in
earlier chapters of this study.

Basic Principles

The proposed model is designed to be politically
feasible rather than theoretically pure. It would be easy to
recommend changes which run counter to political realities
in the United States. For example, a number of countries
have demonstrated an ability to combat terrorism effectively, but largely at a cost in civil liberties that the
American people would be unwilling to pay, given the present
low level of terrorist activity. No available foreign model
can be grafted onto the unique American political, social,
and psychological scene. For a model to be politically
feasible given the current economic environment, it must not
be prohibitively expensive.

A basic principle adopted in developing the proposed
model is that any viable response mechanism must have the
top of its chain of command close enough to the president
both to reflect his wishes and to serve as an educational
tool for him. The president has the power, and perhaps the
duty, to preempt decision making in any crisis involving the

125

national interest. The record indicates clearly that presidents do, in fact, intervene in politically important decisions involving terrorism. Response mechanisms some distance from the White House will tend to be overridden as soon as an important terrorist incident occurs in which the federal interest is paramount.

Unfortunately, if the expertise concerning terrorism is scattered through the federal bureaucracy but the president and his immediate advisers assume control of a terrorist incident, it is improbable that the most appropriate decisions will be made. The first minutes and hours of a terrorist crisis are likely to be the critical ones. Any initial mistakes are apt to be compounded until the situation is beyond favorable resolution. For example, President Nixon's off-the-cuff remarks about the unacceptability of negotiating with terrorists while a high-level government emissary was en route to the Sudan have been regarded by many observers as responsible for the death of Ambassador Noel in Khartoum. The president needs sound advice from the best available sources as soon as a terrorist incident erupts, not days or even hours later.

Presidents also need some familiarity with a subject before they begin making decisions with respect to it. Even President Kennedy, who was very much interested in foreign affairs and who as a senator had become expert in many foreign-policy questions, committed the serious error of authorizing the Bay of Pigs invasion. A response mechanism essentially situated in the White House can provide the president with opportunities to become familiar with various aspects of terrorism before he is required to make life-or-death decisions.

President Carter took a first step in this direction when he created the Special Coordination Committee (SCC) of the National Security Council to handle such matters as crisis management, including terrorism. Immediately under the SCC was the Executive Committee on Terrorism, consisting of representatives of the departments of State, Defense, Justice, Treasury, Transportation, and Energy, and the CIA and the NSC staff. However, these groups were merely coordinating bodies with a short attention span. Members of the executive committee would attend meetings on terrorism at the Executive Office Building, and then return to their departments and agencies to pursue their other duties. The required day-to-day work was still handled by personnel in the departments and agencies with a specific interest in terrorism. When the Iranian hostage crisis erupted, the mechanism was either ignored or proved inadequate to the task.

Another basic principle is that measures taken by the executive branch of the federal government cannot by

themselves solve the problem of coordination between
federal, state, and local governments and agencies. While
some existing problems between these jurisdictions could be
worked out through negotiations, others would best be solved
by legislation. The proposed model, therefore, depends to
some extent on the adoption of some new laws by Congress.

Congressional Actions

In considering what Congress might accomplish
through new legislation, the West German experience is
instructive. West Germany took a giant step toward solving
its jurisdictional problems by adopting legislation making
typical terrorist crimes federal violations, thus bringing
in the federal police, the Bundeskriminalamt. This German
counterpart of the FBI responded by developing the most
complete computer data base concerning terrorism available
in the Western world. Two separate problems are posed for
Congress in trying to use the West German experience.

The first problem is the extent to which the FBI
should be brought into <u>all</u> terrorist incidents within the
United States. Congress has tried unsuccessfully to solve
this problem by defining a terrorist crime. If such a
definition could be agreed upon, it might be possible to
enact legislation enabling or directing the FBI to intervene
in all terrorist incidents. This approach, however, has
consistently failed because no entirely satisfactory
definition of terrorism has yet been devised. Some crimes
can only be differentiated on the basis of motive, and
motives may be difficult to determine until the perpetrators
have been apprehended and all the circumstances established
in a court of law. By then, the response mechanism has
already responded and the question has become academic.

Other approaches are possible, however, and should
be explored. One would be to emulate the West German
example and authorize the FBI to intervene in those types of
crimes typically committed by terrorists. Such legislation
already exists to bring the FBI into all cases of kidnapping, a major terrorist tactic. This legislation could be
extended to include hostage taking, also a major terrorist
tactic closely allied to kidnapping. The FBI currently
becomes involved in all hostage situations involving foreign
official personnel; it would be relatively easy to amplify
existing laws to include all hostage situations.

Legal provisions could be made to involve the FBI in
such other typical crimes committed by terrorists as
bombings, sabotage, and extortion. The legislation proposed
by this study would authorize the FBI to supplement rather
than supersede state and local actions. The FBI would
become involved in these incidents only when requested by

state and local authorities, to minimize the possibilities
for increased administrative Balkanization. Giving the FBI
obligatory jurisdiction over terrorist bombings in New York
City would not make much sense, since the New York Police
Department seems capable of handling threats of this kind.
On the other hand, in smaller communities without trained
manpower and with limited resources, the local authorities
would probably be well advised to request that the FBI take
over bombing incidents.

Another approach would be to draft legislation
enabling the FBI to intervene whenever any crime was
committed by a terrorist group. The attorney general would
be instructed to compile and maintain a list of known
terrorist organizations. Whenever any crime was committed
by one of these groups, the FBI would be authorized to
cooperate fully with the local authorities. The feasibility
of this approach is increased by the fact that terrorist
groups frequently rush to take public credit for their
actions. Publicity is an integral and important part of the
terrorist strategy. Moreover, in the present political and
social climate, it should not be too difficult for the major
sectors of the political spectrum to agree on what constitutes a terrorist group. By contrast, it would have been
very difficult to reach such agreement during the 1960's.

With such legislation in place, the way would be
clear for the FBI to attempt emulating the West German
success with computerized intelligence regarding domestic
terrorist groups. Information in the FBI computer should be
exempted from Freedom of Information Act inquiries if state
and local officials are to be induced to share information
with the federal government. The task facing the FBI would,
however, be more difficult than it was for the West German
Bundeskriminalamt because of the size, diversity, and
complexity of the United States and the highly porous nature
of its borders. Nevertheless, the attempt to duplicate the
West German success appears worth the cost.

Another basic principle is that care must be
exercised by the executive and legislative branches of the
government in fashioning and implementing antiterrorist
measures to make certain that the constitutional rights of
Americans are not curtailed. In the long run, popular
confidence in the government and trust in the rationality of
its actions are the best guarantees that the United States
will not be overrun by domestic terrorism as some other
nations have been. The kind of unconstitutional, illegal
measures undertaken by the Nixon administration would
antagonize many Americans if they were adopted again,
thereby eroding the public support needed to keep terrorism
in check. Where extraordinary measures become necessary, it
is important that the government explain the reasons for its
actions.

Changes in the Executive Branch

The proposed model requires changes in the organization and functions of a number of departments and other segments of the executive branch. These changes are described in the following pages, beginning with the most significant one.

Executive Office of the President

The National Security Council (NSC) should have one senior staff member devoting his full efforts to studying, coordinating, and serving as action officer for terrorism matters. This individual should be on the same administrative level as those NSC staff officials responsible for a major geographic area.

The NSC has never duplicated and should not attempt to duplicate the entire federal bureaucracy. Typically, one individual on the NSC staff follows a specific geographic area (such as the continent of Africa) or a major discipline (international economic problems, for example). This specialist knows personally and coordinates closely with the key personnel in the Department of State, the CIA, the Defense Department, and other agencies concerned with his geographic or functional area.

Despite its comparatively small staff, the NSC can exert great influence in the formulation and implementation of national policy. It is in the interest of the working levels in the various departments and agencies to coordinate closely with the NSC, because of the access it provides to presidential decisions. At the same time, it is necessary for the NSC regional or functional officers to work closely with the experts in the departments and agencies, because of the large number of problems and the prodigious mass of written materials (cables, dispatches, position papers, etc.) that come across their desks.

In practice, therefore, the bureaucracy works both vertically, through the hierarchy of one department or agency, and laterally, between the NSC and the departments and agencies. Its culminating point, the focus of all its efforts, is the effort to have the president adopt a particular policy document. The president can be approached directly by a cabinet officer, such as the secretary of state, only in some instances. Since Kennedy, all major foreignpolicy problems have passed through the NSC mechanism, giving the latter a measure of power which has occasionally been resented but with which it is nevertheless necessary to reckon.

Unfortunately, the NSC has never had a functional expert on terrorism on its staff. Ad hoc groups have been formed from time to time in response to a specific incident, then subsequently dissolved. Moreover, such organizations as the Carter SCC were not functional parts of the NSC, and there were no experts on terrorism within the NSC staff to back up their efforts.

The appointment of a terrorist specialist to a senior position on the NSC staff would help solve a number of major problems evident in the past.

1. It would eliminate Balkanization within the federal government by making the NSC the lead agency in all incidents where the federal interest was paramount. The departments and agencies would still have a major role to play, but they would be operating under the policies and overall direction of the NSC. The president would be kept informed of developments by his national security adviser, while the adviser would depend on the NSC's terrorism expert for background and information on changing developments.

2. Such a structure would place the focus of information where it belongs, next to the source of constitutional power and effective decision making. The decisions made during the first phases of a terrorist incident would then more probably be based on a sophisticated interpretation of the best intelligence. The wide abyss--between those who know and understand and those who make the decisions--characteristic of antiterrorism efforts during the Nixon and the Carter administrations would tend to lessen or even disappear. This proposal assumes that the president has a national security adviser he trusts and on whom he depends, and that the NSC's terrorism expert is the most competent person who can be found for the job.

3. Placing the locus of responsibility within the NSC would serve to tie together the disparate efforts of the many government groups involved in terrorism research and operations. The NSC's terrorism expert would have the political authority and thorough understanding of problems to make certain that everything possible and necessary was being done by the bureaucracy. Because of his proximity to the president, the NSC terrorism expert would be motivated to make certain that the bureaucracy was in a state of readiness to provide him with intelligence and analysis of the highest quality at a moment's notice. Duplication of effort would tend to be eliminated because the NSC would want to have each department and agency concentrate on doing what it did best. The heads of all departments and agencies active in the antiterrorism struggle are members of the NSC; where problems of jurisdiction or coverage developed, they could be handled by discussions between the cabinet officers and directors and the NSC staff. Major issues could easily be brought to the president for his personal decision.

Department of State

Critics of the existing structure have emphasized the need for a major concentration of terrorism experts assigned to a single agency of the government. This agency ought probably to be the Department of State.

Where the new Terrorism Office should be located could be debated at some length. The State Department (the site of the original Working Group on Terrorism), the CIA, and the Justice Department are all possible government units where the office could be located. The CIA has computerized files, excellent facilities, sources of information, and experienced personnel in the field. The Justice Department has legal expertise and the FBI to recommend it. The arguments in favor of locating the Terrorism Office within the State Department seem decisive, however. Most domestic terrorist groups have some foreign-policy objectives such as independence for Puerto Rico or Croatia, or protests against the treatment of Jews by the Soviet Union. No other department or agency is as well equipped by training and inclination to assess the impact of domestic terrorism on foreign-policy objectives. Most terrorist incidents in New York are likely to result from the presence of the United Nations, a State Department responsibility. Most anti-American terrorist incidents overseas are directed against American diplomatic installations, American diplomats, or military personnel assigned to United States diplomatic missions. Furthermore, the State Department is physically close enough to the White House to permit personnel and documents to reach it in a few minutes. By contrast, the CIA is more than a half-hour from the White House by automobile. The State Department is more open to the public than are the CIA, the Justice Department, or the Defense Department's National Security Agency--an important consideration if the services of experts from the private sector are used. At the same time, its physical security arrangements have never been questioned.

The State Department has excellent, secure communications facilities, but it has lagged in computerizing its files. Messages can be transmitted in coded form from any American post overseas and decoded and distributed in the Washington area in minutes. The department has an operations center staffed by representatives of the military services and the CIA, as well as by its own people, with facilities for housing task forces. On the other hand, some money would probably need to be expended to ensure the prompt retrieval of information on terrorism through improved computerization.

The proposed model would require a shift in the focus of the State Department's efforts. Traditionally, the

Working Group on Terrorism was supposed to manage terrorist incidents through the formation of task forces comprised of the WGT staff, the regional bureaus, and representatives of other agencies. Similar task forces but with different personnel would simultaneously be created in the Justice Department, the FAA, and other agencies. However, these task forces have in the past been more advisory than managerial, because decisions were normally made by higher authorities.

Since, under the proposed model, future crises would be managed by the Executive Office of the President, the State Department would no longer have a management function. Its essential role would be to provide the best possible information regarding all important aspects of terrorism.

The new Terrorism Office ought to have a larger staff than the six officers and three secretaries comprising the Working Group on Terrorism. It should include experts from the FBI, the CIA, and the FAA, specialists in international law concerning terrorism, media specialists, and experts in the regional aspects of terrorism. Assuming at least five regional specialists, the Terrorism Office ought to have at least ten officers and an equal number of secretaries and research assistants. The staff should be small but adequate. All staff members should be in one office rather than scattered through the different regional bureaus.

The new Terrorism Office would be the one place in the government where anyone interested in terrorism would go for ideas and information. Other parts of the government would continue to pursue their particular concerns as before, but the fruits of their labors--information, insights, and ideas--would automatically be deposited with the Terrorism Office. One of the office's duties would be to keep in close touch with everyone in the federal government, selected state and local law enforcement officials, and private researchers investigating terrorism. The office would engage in continual informal contacts as well as occasional formal meetings designed to ensure the exchange of ideas between the public and private sectors. The office would be the principal contributor to National Intelligence Estimates and NSC policy documents, which would be handled in the usual way in all other respects.

If such an office existed and functioned as indicated, it would know exactly on whom to call for assistance in any crisis. Experts on terrorism in the United States are not so numerous as to make that task an onerous or impractical one.

Where should such an office be situated within the State Department? As long as terrorism remains a major

concern, it should probably be made a separate office, with
its director a special assistant to the secretary of state.
Alternatively, it might be made a separate entity within the
Office of Intelligence Research (INR). The INR has close
ties with the CIA, is responsible for State's liaison with
the FBI, and maintains a continuing dialogue with the
scholarly community. In addition, it is one of the few
sections of the Department of State not staffed exclusively
by Foreign Service officers, so that more stability could be
maintained than has been the case with the WGT. The problem
would be to make sure that the chief of the Terrorism Office
had free access to the NSC and to the secretary of state.
Such access would be more likely if the organization were
made a separate entity, but it could also be ensured by
careful drafting of its charter.

The creation of a Terrorism Office would be in
addition to whatever other antiterrorism efforts the government is now making. The CIA's experts as well as personnel
in the Justice Department and the FAA would continue to
concentrate on terrorism as before. However, the Terrorism
Office would help the NSC focus the efforts of everyone
involved so as to eliminate duplication and to fill currently existing gaps. The office would be the answer to
Hubbard's criticism that "there is no systematic approach
now extant in the Government for collection, storage,
retrieval, or analysis of relevant data about . . .
[terrorist] crimes."[1] The office would become the government's capacious memory as well as its primary think tank in
all matters involving terrorism.

Central Intelligence Agency

No really major changes would be needed in the
operations of the Central Intelligence Agency. One significant change would be to authorize the CIA to develop
information regarding terrorist groups in the United States.
Most of these groups have either international connections
or a cause outside the United States. The CIA would be
permitted to carry on its operations inside the United
States when: (1) a source outside the United States came to
this country; (2) leads developed overseas permitted an
intelligence breakthrough in the United States; (3) an
organization primarily active overseas undertook activities
inside the United States; and (4) comparable cases worked
out as events required.

Guidelines for the conduct of CIA operations against
terrorists inside the United States would be prepared by the

---

[1]David Hubbard, in Terrorism, Part 1, Hearings,
p. 2976.

NSC, signed by the president, and monitored closely by the NSC's terrorism expert.

The rationale for this change can be stated simply. The CIA has assets with an interest in terrorism which it would not be willing to share with the FBI or any other government agency. These assets might be associated only peripherally with terrorists, but might offer valuable information or insights. The agency should not be required either to jeopardize or to drop these sources while they are in the United States. Moreover, there are groups and individuals with which the CIA can probably be more effective than can the FBI. It would be imprudent for the United States to sacrifice access to invaluable intelligence information as a result of a division-of-labor principle that has worked only indifferently in some fields.

Another, relatively minor, change would be to assign needed personnel to the State Department's Terrorism Office. It would be useful to build up a cadre of personnel with experience working at this level of the antiterrorist effort.

Department of Justice

Under the proposed new model structure, the Department of Justice would have some added responsibilities. One would be to prepare and maintain a list of terrorist organizations active inside the United States. As already indicated, this task is likely to be politically sensitive. It should be carried out in a pragmatic rather than a doctrinaire fashion. This endeavor, like all others, should be monitored closely by the NSC.

In addition, the FBI would have the responsibility of assisting state and local agencies in dealing with terrorist incidents. This assistance should probably go beyond the usual cooperation between the local FBI office and the local authorities. The FBI should develop a small, elite group of terrorism experts able to move swiftly to the site of any terrorist incident in the United States, when requested to do so by the local authorities. These experts would be senior and skilled enough to take control of local forces upon request. The team should be large enough to be capable of undertaking all phases of the counterterrorist operation, together with local FBI personnel, when the local forces are inadequate for the job. However, where local authorities want to retain command, the FBI would assist only to the extent that was requested and that the FBI itself considered prudent. For instance, an untrained local police chief might want the FBI contingent to engage in some reckless action, but the FBI would have the right to refuse the request.

Department of Defense

Department of Defense terrorism activities would remain the same, with two exceptions. The Defense Intelligence Agency would be under the same constraints to work under the direction of the NSC in all areas dealing with terrorism as would the other intelligence and operating agencies. Otherwise, the DIA would operate as it has in the past.

A more important change would be the creation of an elite, mobile antiterrorist unit that could be dispatched on short notice to any place in the world. The failure of the Iranian hostage rescue attempt demonstrates the inadvisability of trying to put together an ad hoc team drawn from a number of services, in response to a particular crisis. As already indicated, the joint nature of the Iranian operation contributed heavily to its failure. The fact that equipment had to be borrowed was also a contributing factor.

The new antiterrorist unit might be staffed by members drawn from all of the services, but would be under the control of the Joint Chiefs of Staff rather than one of the individual services. Members of this Antiterrorist Tactical Command (ATC) would be encouraged to view it as their primary home in the service. They would train together, work together, and become thoroughly expert in all those terrorist situations where the use of force is unavoidable. The decision to use force, and therefore the Antiterrorist Tactical Command, would only be made by the president, following recommendation by the NSC.

Apart from being a homogeneous unit, the ATC would be large enough to cope with Iran-type situations. The force used in the failed Iran rescue operation consisted of 200 men, not counting the aircraft and helicopter crews. Two hundred men would seem to be the minimum for an antiterrorist tactical force, with twice that number probably more advisable.

To the extent possible, the force would have its own aircraft, including C-130's and helicopters. Efficiency would be enhanced by having aircraft crews and force members working together regularly.

Federal Aviation Administration

Together with the departments of State and Justice, the FAA has been one of the lead agencies in a number of terrorist incidents. FAA jurisdiction begins as soon as a plane's doors close and continues for as long as the plane is in American air space. Before the plane's doors close,

the FBI is responsible, together with the local police. If
the plane leaves American air space, the State Department
takes over.

In the proposed model structure, the FAA would no
longer play a lead agency role. Only the NSC would be
considered a lead agency. The FAA would continue to
contribute its information and general expertise to managing
a hijacking incident, but its command role would be superseded by the NSC. The FAA's communications system would
still be needed in any skyjacking crisis, but information
from FAA headquarters would be patched into the NSC offices
where the command task force would be working.

Other Departments and Agencies

Generally, some of the agencies and departments
which participated in the State Department's Working Group
on Terrorism would not be as much involved under the
proposed model structure. The Agency for International
Development and the Arms Control and Disarmament Agency have
only a peripheral interest in terrorism and would normally
be represented by the State Department. Other agencies with
only a minimal interest in terrorism include the Department
of Commerce, the Department of Energy, the Department of the
Treasury, the Immigration and Naturalization Service, the
Center for Disease Control, and the Nuclear Regulatory
Commission. There is little reason for these agencies to
have to participate in regular, formal meetings on the
subject of terrorism. Members of the new Terrorism Office
would, however, maintain contact with all of these departments and agencies to make certain that concerned personnel
were familiar with the roles they might be called on to play
in a terrorist crisis.

Some of these organizations might occasionally have
a major role to discharge. If, as happened recently, it is
feared that terrorists are about to enter the United States,
the Immigration and Naturalization Service, the Coast Guard,
and the Customs Service would have to be briefed and
assigned their proper functions. In the case of these and
other peripheral departments and agencies, the NSC, knowing
exactly what their capabilities were, could commit their
resources where they were most needed in a crisis. There
would be no need to make regular antiterrorism meetings
time-consuming and unwieldy by involving large numbers of
only peripherally related agencies.

The information obtained by the National Security
Agency constitutes basic, reliable, and extremely important
intelligence. However, no useful purpose would be served by
involving the NSA in policy meetings concerning terrorism.
The NSC needs only to know the National Security Agency's

capabilities and problems in this field and to keep it informed about the targets of interest.

The other agencies which were part of the Working Group on Terrorism but which have not been discussed in this chapter can be placed in the same category as the NSA.

The Legislative Branch

The model structure proposed would not require congressional sanction, since it does not involve the creation of a major new organizational entity. Congress does have the power of the purse, but the amounts needed to fund the new governmental activities would be comparatively small. In cases such as that of the Antiterrorist Tactical Command, no budgetary line item would appear.

Even so, it would be prudent to attempt to make Congress a partner in the struggle against terrorism. The groups working against terrorism need to develop a knowledgeable constituency. Virtually every part of the executive branch has its friends and defenders in Congress, and those concerned with terrorism cannot be an exception.

Thus far, the study of terrorism in Congress has been assigned to such groups as the House Subcommittee on Civil and Constitutional Rights, the House Committee on Internal Security, the House Subcommittee on Aviation, and the Senate Committee on Governmental Affairs. It would be preferable to have just one entity in each legislative body handle all aspects of terrorism, rather than having several committees and subcommittees considering problems of terrorism from their necessarily parochial points of view. One solution would be to have the administration lobby for the creation of oversight committees that would include members interested in both the national and the international aspects of terrorism.

The Structure in Practice

The rationale underlying the proposed model structure is to bond the response mechanism into a unified, coherent entity both carrying out the wishes of the president and serving as an educational resource for him. It may be useful to describe the manner in which the response structure would operate, or would have operated, in real-world situations. The examples discussed below involve: (1) domestic groups attacking domestic targets; (2) domestic groups attacking a domestic target with the incident then moving overseas; (3) transnational groups attacking a domestic target; and (4) foreign groups attacking an American target overseas.

Domestic Group Attacking a Domestic Target

One example cited earlier was the seizure of the Islamic Center (mosque) and the B'nai B'rith building in Washington, D.C., in January, 1977, by a group of Hanafi Muslims. According to one account of the incident:

> Nobody knew what to do. The F.B.I. had one idea. The D.C. police had another. The Secret Service had a third. If it hadn't been for the Muslim Ambassadors they'd have been chucking bodies out the windows.[2]

The District of Columbia police had no training for this kind of emergency, and attempts by the FBI to provide them with a crash course in storming buildings held by terrorists were ineffective. Eventually, the incident was brought to a successful end through the mediation of three Muslim ambassadors stationed in Washington.

The outcome of the incident might have been the same under the proposed model response structure, but at least the comedy of errors could have been avoided. The FBI and the Secret Service would have been required to speak with one voice, the voice of the president transmitted through the NSC.[3] The Islamic Center is the property of the Islamic embassies in Washington and therefore a federal responsibility. The federal agencies would have pursued the course decided upon by the president, the NSC, and its terrorism expert, backed by the State Department's Terrorism Office.

Jurisdiction over the B'nai B'rith building would have remained with the District of Columbia during the incident. It is most unlikely that the Hanafi Muslims would have appeared on anyone's list of terrorist organizations, since they had been a peaceful religious group until the takeover. Under the proposed legislation dealing with terrorist crimes--hostage taking, in this case--the FBI would have been authorized to take over management of the crisis if requested to do so by the local authorities. Given the obvious lack of preparedness on the part of the District police, the major federal interest, and the

---

[2]Gregory F. Rose, "The Terrorists Are Coming," Politics Today, July/August 1978, p. 52.

[3]It is not suggested that the president must necessarily become involved in such or any other terrorist incident. The presidential decision may simply be one to have the NSC handle the problem. However, in a major incident such as this one, the president, being responsible for federal actions, would have to be consulted.

international implications, it seems likely that the local
authorities would have asked the FBI to take over.

It is not possible to predict how this cohesiveness
of authority would have affected the outcome of the incident. It seems probable that less time would have been lost
in bringing the ambassadors in to negotiate a settlement.

Domestic Group Attacking a Domestic
Target, Then Moving Overseas

An example of an attack on a domestic target by a
domestic group with eventual international ramifications was
the hijacking of the TWA airliner by Croatian nationalists
in September, 1976.[4] The plane was seized by the Croatians
in New York, where the incident was first the responsibility
of the FBI and the New York Police Department. Once the
plane's doors closed, responsibility devolved on the FAA
until the plane entered Canadian airspace, causing the State
Department to become the lead agency. According to one
participant in managing the incident, the "responsibility
for the action bounced around the Government like a floating
crap game."[5] Confusion as to who was in charge at any given
moment could have been avoided under the proposed model
structure; the NSC would have been in command throughout.

Having the NSC act on behalf of the president would
have had another advantage in this particular case. As soon
as the hijacked aircraft landed at Paris's Orly Field, the
French shot out its tires and adopted a policy of no
compromise. Whatever may be the merits of such a policy in
the abstract, it was inappropriate in this case because the
Croatian demands had all been met by the American government
and press. The American ambassador in Paris had a very
difficult time convincing the French that he should be
permitted to speak with the Croatians. The Croatians on the
plane did not know that they had been successful. Faced
with a French ultimatum to surrender without discussion, and
believing that their hijacking had been to no avail, they
might well have sacrificed themselves and the plane's
passengers in order to publicize their cause. The NSC, had
it been in direct charge of the incident, could have
informed the president of the problem with the French, which
a phone call from the White House could have solved. This

---

[4]Brian M. Jenkins, in An Act to Combat International
Terrorism, Hearings, p. 108. While the Croatians were
fighting for an objective outside the United States, they
were American subjects and have to be regarded as a domestic
terrorist group.

[5]Ibid.

course of action would have been much more difficult to take for the comparatively low-level managers of the incident, who were physically remote from the White House. As soon as the American ambassador was able to tell the hijackers that their publicity demands had been met, they surrendered.

Transnational Group Attacking a Domestic Target

There have been few examples of attacks on domestic targets by transnational terrorists. The Puerto Rican nationalists are American citizens who want a change in the political and economic relationship between the United States and Puerto Rico. Attacks by the Jewish Defense League have generally been against Soviet targets in the United States. The Croatians who have undertaken terrorist acts in the United States have either been American citizens or resident aliens. Transnational groups such as the IRA have viewed the United States as a source of funds and arms and appear to have been careful not to attack domestic targets here.

One recent example may have been the reported attempt by terrorists headed by "Carlos the Jackal" to enter the United States to assassinate key American officials.[6] The terrorists were allegedly dispatched on this mission by Libya's Colonel Qaddafi.[7]

This example is difficult to analyze for a number of reasons. It is not entirely clear whether the dispatch of "hit teams" actually took place or was merely contemplated, or whether the entire affair was part of a psychological warfare campaign being waged by the United States against the Libyan regime. Assuming that the threat was genuine, the full publicity given it was curious. The questions posed by this "incident" may not be answered until historians are able to study the relevant declassified documents.

However, the response mechanism used to cope with the perceived threat was essentially the one proposed in

---

[6]"The Kaddafi Hit Squad at Large?" Newsweek, 14 December 1981, pp. 36-37; David M. Alpern, "Coping with a Plot to Kill the President," Newsweek, 21 December 1981, pp. 16-17; "Libyan Assassins Now After Reagan?" U.S. News & World Report, 14 December 1981, p. 5; "Why Reagan Moved Against Libya's Qadhafi," "A President Under Wraps," and "A Broker in Global Terror," U.S. News & World Report, 21 December 1981, pp. 10-11.

[7]No distinction is made here between "transnational" and "international" terrorism.

this study. The usual terrorism response structure was bypassed in favor of a series of meetings between the president and the NSC. A number of agencies outside the NSC were involved in the ensuing countermeasures, but the decisions were made by the president himself. One indication of the role he played is the fact that he acted as a spokesman for the nation concerning the affair, instead of leaving the matter to the White House or State Department press spokesmen. The NSC mechanism did not include the terrorism expert called for in this study, but representatives of those departments and agencies with the greatest expertise on terrorism were present.[8] Decisions with respect to the Libyan hit-team problem were made, as recommended here, by the president after he received advice from the NSC and experts in the field.

It is also difficult to determine whether the course pursued by the government was the best one available under the circumstances. If the threat was real, information regarding it must have been acquired from a very sensitive source, probably electronic intelligence or an American close to the ruling circles in Libya. Plausible and essentially confirmatory evidence from Libyan exile sources was eventually released. It seems highly unlikely that the American government would have moved so strongly on the basis only of the reports released to the press and the public. Even the best information from a "controlled" foreign source is almost always labeled as "probably true" rather than as factually correct. Having claimed that Qaddafi had dispatched trained terrorists to the United States to assassinate high officials, the Reagan administration, faced with some skepticism, had to present some evidence but could not release its principal, highly sensitive information.

If this speculation is correct, the mishandling may have been due to the absence in the NSC family of a first-rate terrorism expert. The same results could have been obtained with fewer questions being posed by notifying all personnel in a position to intercept the terrorists--including Customs, INS, and the Border Patrol--of the existence of the plot, giving the names and descriptions of the terrorists, as was actually done later. The news would, of course, have leaked out. The administration would reluctantly have confirmed it but would have refused to divulge any of its sources. This method would have been somewhat

---

[8]James Kelly, Douglas Brew, and Adam Zagorin, "Searching for Hit Teams," *Time*, 21 December 1981, pp. 16-20; George J. Church, Laurence I. Barrett, and Frank Melville, "Some Sanctions That May Not Work," *Time*, 21 December 1981, pp. 24-26.

more credible, would have warned the terrorists that they were expected, and would have aroused American and foreign public opinion against Qaddafi.

What appears to have happened in this case is that the administration instinctively adopted the best possible response structure to cope with the threat of the Libyan-controlled terrorists. However, the input that might have been provided by a terrorism expert on the NSC staff and a concentration of experts on terrorism in the federal bureaucracy was missing. Thus, mistakes may have been made that could have been avoided.

Terrorist Group Attacking an American Target Overseas

The latest major attack of this sort occurred too recently to be mentioned in earlier chapters of this study. On December 17, 1981, members of the Italian Red Brigades kidnapped United States Brigadier General James Dozier from his home in Verona, Italy. Dozier was vice commander of NATO land forces in southern Europe. The announced purpose of the abduction was to place Dozier on trial in a "people's court" for his "crimes" as a NATO commander. The call of the Red Brigades for war against NATO and for meting out proletarian justice to Dozier also allied them closely with West Germany's Red Army Faction and with other terrorist groups in Europe.[9]

The primary responsibility for the release of Dozier lay with the Italian authorities. After a decade marked by an almost complete lack of success, as exemplified by the Aldo Moro kidnapping and murder, the Italians have gradually learned to cope with terrorism. In May, 1980, the Italian police captured the leader of the Red Brigades in Turin, enabling them to decimate the terrorists' organization in Turin and Genoa.[10] The capture of other members of the Red Brigades enabled the Italian police to find and release Dozier unharmed.

The U.S. response mechanism appears to have worked well in this incident. It is not possible for an outsider to know how effective the American advisers sent to Italy to work with the local police were. The president condemned the Red Brigades but said nothing that would be likely to cause Dozier's death.

---

[9]Kim Rogal and Elaine Sciolino, "The Kidnapped U.S. General," Newsweek, 28 December 1981, p. 46.

[10]John Brecher, with Loren Jenkins, "Joining Forces Against Terrorism" Newsweek, 2 June 1980, p. 50.

The outcome of this incident contrasts sharply with the results of the Khartoum incident described in detail in chapter 2. Sudanese terrorists seized a number of diplomats in the Saudi Arabian embassy in Khartoum, demanding the release of hundreds of political prisoners around the world. The Nixon administration dispatched a senior State Department official to the Sudan to seek the release of Ambassador Noel and Deputy Chief of Mission Moore. Before the State Department's negotiator could arrive, President Nixon announced at a press conference that the United States would not give in to blackmail. Noel and Moore were shot by the terrorists, who then surrendered to the Sudanese authorities. In this case, the American government's response structure performed as if one end did not know what the other end was doing.

Like the Italian police, the United States appears to have learned a great deal about how to cope with terrorism. Organizational and substantive problems remain, however. The streamlined, more cohesive organization proposed in this study would help solve the substantive problems by eliminating administrative fragmentation, by providing the government with a concentration of experts, and by bringing knowledge and political responsibility closer together.

Chart of the Model

Decisions	THE PRESIDENT
	NATIONAL SECURITY COUNCIL

Primary Adviser	NSC STAFF'S "TERRORISM EXPERT"

Central Working Level Organization	STATE DEPARTMENT'S "TERRORISM OFFICE"

Additional
Governmental
Resources:
Intelligence (N),
Operational (O)

CIA (N, O)	FBI (N, O)		
NSA (N)	DIA (N)	JCS (O)	
FAA (O, N)	INS (O)		
CUSTOMS SERVICE (O)	COAST GUARD (O)		
POSTAL SERVICE (O)			

Groups
with
Peripheral
Interest in
Terrorism

AGENCY FOR INTERNATIONAL DEVELOPMENT
ARMS CONTROL AND DISARMAMENT AGENCY
DEPARTMENTS OF ENERGY AND TRANSPORTATION
CENTER FOR DISEASE CONTROL   NUCLEAR REGULATORY COMMISSION
OMB   U.S. MISSION TO THE UN   U.S. MARSHAL'S OFFICE

Departments Not Shown on Chart Because Represented on NSC	DEPARTMENT OF STATE DEPARTMENT OF JUSTICE DEPARTMENT OF THE TREASURY

Private Sector Resources	THINK TANKS INDIVIDUAL SCHOLARS

NOTE: The chain of command runs from level 2 to levels 3, 4, and 5.

APPENDIX

SOURCES OF INFORMATION AND DATA ON TERRORISM

Governmental Sources

Until recently, the Central Intelligence Agency (CIA) published analyses of various problems and events for the benefit of the general public. These analyses represented attempts to delete all classified materials from official reports in order to provide academicians, journalists, businessmen, and other interested citizens with information that would be essentially correct without the wealth of supporting detail from classified sources found in original reports.

The CIA has recently discontinued the practice of preparing such analyses. According to CIA spokesman Dale Peterson:

> It took manpower to start with a classified report and try to produce something meaningful in an unclassified fashion. . . . Our primary responsibility is to provide U.S. government policy makers with the best intelligence product we are capable of producing. We saw that a lot of analysts' time was spent preparing these unclassified analytical pieces.[1]

Another reason for discontinuance of the CIA series on subjects such as terrorism and estimates of future Soviet oil production was the desire of its director, William J. Casey, to have the agency maintain a "low profile."[2] In the same spirit, background briefings for journalists concerning foreign political, economic, military, and scientific developments have been sharply curtailed.

Scholars will, therefore, have to do without CIA materials in the immediate future. It was noted in chapter 1 that CIA analysts classify terrorist acts according to

---

[1]Associated Press, "CIA to Curtail Data for Public Use," Washington Post, 11 November 1981, p. 12.

[2]Ibid.

whether they were carried out by basically autonomous nonstate actors or by individuals and groups controlled by some sovereign state. This classification, however, creates so many problems that the CIA's public analyses of terrorism have been less useful than they would probably have been if a less subjective method of classification had been adopted.

The State Department is one of the lead agencies in the fight against terrorism. All of the information that the department wishes the public to have is published in the Department of State Bulletin. This monthly publication includes speeches and policy statements, and is available from the Superintendent of Documents, U.S. Government Printing Office, Washington, D.C., 20402, on a subscription basis. This information source is important because it provides the definitive United States government position with respect to terrorism. The Foreign Service Journal, the organ of the Foreign Service, is of value to any researcher who wants to know what Foreign Service officers think about the American no-ransom policy.

The primary lead agency for dealing with domestic terrorism is the Federal Bureau of Investigation (FBI). Materials dealing with terrorism are sometimes found in the FBI Law Enforcement Bulletin, available from the Federal Bureau of Investigation, U.S. Department of Justice, Washington, D.C., 20535. This bulletin is also available on microfiche from the National Criminal Justice Reference Service (P.O. Box 24036, S.W. Post Office, Washington, D.C., 20024).

The National Criminal Justice Reference Service has available, also on microfiche, a variety of materials from foreign police sources. The file of Police Chief, the periodical of the International Association of Chiefs of Police, is also on microfiche. Police Chief, published at 11 Firstfield Road, Gaithersburg, Maryland, 20760, is an important source of information on the views of state and local law enforcement authorities.

The National Criminal Justice Reference Service and the National Institute of Law Enforcement and Criminal Justice also publish periodical supplements of annotated bibliographies dealing with terrorism.

Among the most useful sources available are the published accounts of the many congressional hearings held on the subject of terrorism during the past decade. The great advantage of a congressional hearing is that its witnesses are not limited to reading a prepared statement. The witnesses must also answer questions put to them by legislators from both ends of the political spectrum. Such questioning elicits more detail than would be provided if the witnesses were limited to prepared statements.

Another method often used by the federal government to develop new ideas and collect facts is to create a special commission to investigate a particular problem. The National Advisory Committee on Criminal Justice and Standards was formed by the Law Enforcement Assistance Administration in the spring of 1975. It was headed by Brendan T. Byrne, governor of New Jersey. The resulting Report of the Task Force on Disorders and Terrorism contains more than 650 pages of useful materials, including analyses of the efforts of several foreign nations to combat terrorism.

The Library of Congress issues Subject Catalogs four times a year, listing new acquisitions that have been processed and are available for reading. Many of these acquisitions have been prepared by organizations and writers outside the United States.

Journals published by elements of the American armed forces also include articles and data on terrorism. One example of these is the Air University Review.

One problem with almost all of the professional sources just enumerated is that the views represented are almost exclusively those of the federal government. One exception is the congressional hearings, where a variety of views is expressed. Another exception is a report by the Department of State denying the existence of international terrorism. According to that report, all that exists is a diversity of national dissident groups, some of which use terrorism to advance their purposes.[3] In general, however, to obtain access to something other than the "party line," it is necessary to consult other types of sources.

Nongovernmental Sources

The Rand Corporation is quasi-governmental: it is a private corporation which earns most of its money through government contracts. The papers and books issued by the Rand Corporation are designed to facilitate the exchange of ideas among those who share Rand's research interests. Brian M. Jenkins is Rand's principal expert on terrorism and has published some 30 papers on the subject. A list of Rand publications dealing with terrorism is available from the Rand Corporation, 2100 "M" Street, N.W., Washington, D.C., 20037, or from the Rand Corporation's west coast office in Santa Monica, California.

---

[3]Irving L. Horowitz, Unicorns and Terrorists (Washington, D.C.: U.S. Department of State, 1976).

Virtually all significant terrorist acts are reported by those American newspapers normally covering important world news. The New York Times and the Washington Post are two such newspapers. The Times coverage is usually complete, while the Post may be consulted primarily for its interpretative coverage of the Washington scene.

After a terrorist incident has been reported in the daily press, many national periodicals also cover it. Publications such as Time, Newsweek, U.S. News & World Report, and others present usually condensed versions of the incident, with the benefit of somewhat more time in which to research and write their accounts. The Economist of London also provides reasonably complete coverage of world terrorism. Many other periodicals offer in-depth analyses. One of the periodicals that appears to have covered the subject thoroughly is the New York Times Magazine, but many others--Harper's, National Review, and Security World--include articles of interest. For skyjacking and countermeasures, Aviation Week and Space Technology is one of the best sources. Magazines such as Science, 81 and Next (now defunct) have featured articles dealing with new technology as it impinges on the terrorist threat.

Of the various specialized journals, Terrorism: An International Journal, edited by Yonah Alexander, is the one most relevant to the study of terrorism. It began publication in 1978, and has devoted entire issues to a particular country or problem. Much of the work it publishes is highly theoretical and deficient in factual content. Security World frequently includes articles dealing with antiterrorism measures and equipment. Periodicals such as the Poor Man's Armorer carry a great deal of information regarding how lethal weapons can be constructed in one's home workshop; the information gives individuals and groups trying to cope with terrorism some idea of what they are facing.

Much of the material about terrorism available in newspapers and periodicals is brought together in Current News, prepared by the News Clipping and Analysis Service of the U.S. Air Force, acting as agent for the Department of Defense. This service has issued special editions dealing exclusively with terrorism in recent years.

The 1980-1981 Subject Guide to Books in Print lists nearly one hundred books on the subject of terrorism.[4] The Library of Congress collection is much larger, since it includes foreign books and those now out of print. Scores of books dealing with terrorism are published every year. However, relatively few of these concern the United States' response mechanism. Moreover, many of the books go over the same ground, using essentially the same materials.

---

[4]Subject Guide to Books in Print, 1980-1981 (New York: R. R. Bowker, 1980).

SELECTED BIBLIOGRAPHY

Alexander, Yonah; Browne, Marjorie Ann; and James, Allan S.,
    eds. Control of Terrorism: International Docu-
    ments. New York: Crane Russak, 1979.

Alpern, David M. "Coping with a Plot to Kill the President."
    Newsweek, 21 December 1981, pp. 16-17, 19.

Apple, R. W., Jr. In The Watergate Hearings: Break-In and
    Cover-Up, pp. 61-67. Edited by the New York Times.
    New York: Viking Press, 1973.

Aris, Stephen. "Terror in the Land of the Basques." New
    York Times Magazine, 4 May 1980, pp. 82-93.

Associated Press. "CIA to Curtail Data for Public Use."
    Washington Post, 11 November 1981, p. 12.

_____. "Italy Won't Talk with Terrorists." New York
    Times, 14 July 1981, p. 3.

_____. "Red Brigades Sentence Victim to Death." Dallas
    Morning News, 11 July 1981, p. 3.

Bailyn, Bernard; Davis, David Brian; Donald, David Herbert;
    Thomas, John L.; Wiebe, Robert H.; and Wood, Gordon
    S. The Great Republic: A History of the American
    People. Boston: Little, Brown and Co., 1977.

Bell, J. Bowyer. A Time of Terror. New York: Basic Books, 1978.

Bishop, Joseph W., Jr. "Law in the Control of Terrorism and
    Insurrection: The British Laboratory Experience." Law
    and Contemporary Problems 42 (Spring 1978):140-202.

Blackstone Reports. "Terrorism in Italy: A New Dimension."
    Security Management, November 1978, pp. 42-43.

Blechman, Barry. "The Consequences of Israeli Reprisals: An
    Assessment." Ph.D. dissertation, Georgetown Univer-
    sity, 1971.

149

_____. "The Impact of Israel's Reprisals on Behavior of the Bordering Arab Nations Directed at Israel." _Journal of Conflict Resolution_ 16 (June 1972): 155-81.

Blei, Herman. "Terrorism, Domestic and International: The West German Experience." In _Disorders and Terrorism: Report of the Task Force on Disorders and Terrorism_, pp. 497-506. Washington, D.C.: National Advisory Committee on Criminal Justice Standards and Goals, 1976.

Bolz, Francis A., Jr. "Hostage Confrontation and Rescue." In _Terrorism: Threat, Reality, Response_, pp. 393-404. Edited by Robert Kupperman and Darrell Trent. Stanford, Calif.: Hoover Institution Press of Stanford University, 1979.

Brecher, John, with Jenkins, Loren. "Joining Forces Against Terrorism." _Newsweek_, 2 June 1980, p. 50.

"A Broker in Global Terror." _U.S. News & World Report_, 21 December 1981, p. 11.

Brown, Richard H. "Books and Bombs." _Publisher's Weekly_, 23 January 1981, pp. 81-86.

"Can the Turks Unite Against Terror?" _Economist_ (London), 26 July 1980, pp. 45-46.

Caplow, Theodore. _Sociology_. 2nd ed. Englewood Cliffs, N.J.: Prentice-Hall, 1975.

Church, George J.; Barrett, Laurence I.; and Melville, Frank. "Some Sanctions That May Not Work." _Time_, 21 December 1981, pp. 24-26.

Civiletti, Benjamin R. "Testimony." In _Federal Capabilities in Crisis Management and Terrorism_. Hearings Before the Subcommittee on Civil and Constitutional Rights, House of Representatives, 95th Congress, 2nd Sess. Washington, D.C.: Government Printing Office, 1978.

Clyne, P. _Anatomy of Skyjacking_. London: Abelard-Schuman, 1973.

Collins, Larry. "Combating Nuclear Terrorism." _New York Times Magazine_, 14 December 1980, pp. 36-39.

Cooper, H. H. A. "Terrorism and the Intelligence Function." In _Contemporary Terrorism: Selected Readings_, pp. 180-92. Edited by John D. Elliott and Leslie K. Gibson. Gaithersburg, Md.: International Association of Chiefs of Police, 1978.

_____. "Terrorism and the Media." In Terrorism: Inter-
disciplinary Perspectives, pp. 141-56. Edited by
Yonah Alexander and Seymour Maxwell Finger. New
York: John Jay Press, 1977.

Crozier, Brian, ed. Annual of Power and Conflict, 1978-79.
London: Institute for the Study of Conflict, 1979.

Dean, John. "Memorandum for the Attorney General, September
18, 1970." In Big Brother and the Holding Company:
The World Behind Watergate, pp. 329-32. Palo Alto,
Calif.: Ramparts Press, 1974.

Demirsar, Metin. "Turkey's Generals Curb Terrorism." Wall
Street Journal, 17 October 1980, p. 35.

Drinan, Robert F. "Comments." In Federal Capabilities in
Crisis Management and Terrorism. Hearings Before
the Subcommittee on Civil and Constitutional Rights,
House of Representatives, 95th Congress, 2nd Sess.
Washington, D.C.: Government Printing Office, 1978.

Drogin, Robert. "Newark Is Seeking Additional Water as Mains
Burst." Washington Post, 8 July 1981, p. A-8.

Elbrick, C. Burke. "Statement." In Terrorism, Part 2.
Hearings Before the Committee on Internal Security,
House of Representatives, 93rd Congress, 2nd Sess.
Washington, D.C.: Government Printing Office, 1974.

Ellis, Harry B. "The Arab-Israeli Conflict Today." In The
United States and the Middle East, pp. 133-40.
Edited by Georgiana G. Stevens. New York: American
Assembly, Columbia University, 1964.

Evans, A. E. "Aircraft Hijacking--What Is Being Done?" In
International Terrorism and Political Crime, pp.
36-45. Springfield, Ill.: Charles C. Thomas, 1975.

Evans, Ernest. Calling a Truce to Terror: The American
Response to International Terrorism. Westport,
Conn.: Greenwood Press, 1979.

Evans, Rowland, and Novak, Robert. The Reagan Revolution.
New York: E. P. Dutton, 1981.

Fields, Louis G., Jr. "Terrorism: Summary of Applicable
United States and International Law." In Legal and
Other Aspects of Terrorism, pp. 9-28. Edited by
E. Nobles Lowe and Harry D. Shargel. New York: Prac-
ticing Law Institute, 1979.

Fly, Claude L. "Testimony." In Terrorism, Part 3.
    Hearings Before the Committee on Internal Security,
    House of Representatives, 93rd Congress, 2nd Sess.
    Washington, D.C.: Government Printing Office, 1974.

Franks, Lucinda. "The Seeds of Terror." New York Times
    Magazine, 22 November 1981, pp. 34-59, 72-76.

Frederickson, George M. White Supremacy: A Comparative
    Study in American and South African History. New
    York: Oxford University Press, 1981.

Gavzer, Bernard. "Could His Life Have Been Saved?" Wash-
    ington Post Parade, 12 July 1981, pp. 14-15.

Graham, Bradley. "20 Injured by Bomb at U.S. Base." Wash-
    ington Post, 1 September 1981, p. A-13.

Grosman, Brian A. "Dissent and Disorder in Canada." In
    Disorders and Terrorism: Report of the Task Force
    on Disorders and Terrorism, pp. 479-96. Washington,
    D.C.: National Advisory Committee on Criminal Justice
    Standards and Goals, 1976.

"The Growing Danger of Terrorism in the U.S." Business
    Week, 24 December 1979, p. 51.

Gwertzman, Bernard. "Haig Says Teheran Will Not Get Arms."
    New York Times, 29 January 1981, p. 1.

Hacker, Frederick J. "Testimony." In Terrorism, Part 1.
    Hearings Before the Committee on Internal Security,
    House of Representatives, 93rd Congress, 2nd Sess.
    Washington, D.C.: Government Printing Office, 1974.

Haldeman, H. R. "Memorandum to Huston: Domestic Intelli-
    gence Review, July 14, 1970." In Big Brother and
    the Holding Company: The World Behind Watergate,
    pp. 326-30. Palo Alto, Calif.: Ramparts Press, 1974.

Harris. F. Gentry. "Testimony." In Terrorism, Part 1.
    Hearings Before the Committee on Internal Security,
    House of Representatives, 93rd Congress, 2nd Sess.
    Washington, D.C.: Government Printing Office, 1974.

Heren, Louis. "Curbing Terrorism." Atlas World Press
    Review, January 1978, pp. 31-35.

Hersh, Seymour M. "Exposing the Libyan Link: The Qaddafi
    Connection, Part 2." New York Times Magazine,
    28 June 1981, pp. 32-49.

_____. "The Qaddafi Connection: Part 1." New York Times Magazine, 21 June 1981, pp. 52-72.

Hoffacker, Lewis. "Statement." In Terrorism, Part 2. Hearings Before the Committee on Internal Security, House of Representatives, 93rd Congress, 2nd Sess. Washington, D.C.: Government Printing Office, 1974.

Holden, Constance. "Study of Terrorism Emerging as an International Endeavor." Science 203 (5 January 1979): 33-35.

Homer, Frederick D. "Terror in the United States: Three Perspectives." In The Politics of Terrorism, pp. 390-96. Edited by Michael Stohl. New York: Marcel Dekker, 1979.

Hoover, J. Edgar. "Memorandum from the Director of the FBI: FBI Disruption of the Black Panthers, May 11, 1970." In Big Brother and the Holding Company: The World Behind Watergate, pp. 317-19. Palo Alto, Calif.: Ramparts Press, 1974.

Horner, Charles. "The Facts About Terrorism." Commentary 69 (June 1980):40-45.

Horowitz, Irving L. Unicorns and Terrorists. Washington, D.C.: U.S. Department of State, 1976.

Hurewitz, J. C. "The Middle East: A Year of Turmoil." In Foreign Affairs: America and the World, 1980, pp. 540-77. Edited by William P. Bundy. New York: Pergamon Press, 1981.

Huston, Tom Charles. "Decision Memorandum, July 15, 1970." In Big Brother and the Holding Company: The World Behind Watergate, pp. 327-28. Palo Alto, Calif.: Ramparts Press, 1974.

_____. "Operational Restraints on Intelligence Collection." In Big Brother and the Holding Company: The World Behind Watergate, pp. 321-25. Palo Alto, Calif.: Ramparts Press, 1974.

Jenkins, Brian M. Embassies Under Siege. Santa Monica, Calif.: Rand Corporation, January 1981.

_____. "International Terrorism: A Balance Sheet." In Contemporary Terrorism: Selected Readings, pp. 241-50. Edited by John D. Elliott and Leslie K. Gibson. Gaithersburg, Md.: International Association of Chiefs of Police, 1978.

_____. The Study of Terrorism: Definitional Problems. Santa Monica, Calif.: Rand Corporation, December 1980.

_____. Terrorism in the 1980s. Santa Monica, Calif.: Rand Corporation, December 1980.

_____. Terrorism in the United States. Santa Monica, Calif.: Rand Corporation, May 1980.

_____. "Testimony." In An Act to Combat International Terrorism. Hearings Before the Committee on Governmental Affairs, Senate, 95th Congress, 2nd Sess. Washington, D.C.: Government Printing Office, 1978.

Jenkins, Brian M., and Johnson, J. International Terrorism: A Chronology, 1968-1974. Santa Monica, Calif.: Rand Corporation, March 1975.

_____. International Terrorism: A Chronology, 1974 Supplement. Santa Monica, Calif.: Rand Corporation, February 1976.

Jenkins, Brian M.; Tanham, George; Weinstein, Eleanor; and Sullivan, Gerald. U.S. Preparation for Future Low-Level Conflict. Santa Monica, Calif.: Rand Corporation, July 1977.

Johnson, Haynes. "Ford, Carter Unite on Mideast." Washington Post, 12 October 1981, pp. A-1, A-3.

"The Kaddafi Hit Squad at Large?" Newsweek, 14 December 1981, pp. 36-37.

Kelly, James. "Statement." In Terrorism, Part 1. Hearings Before the Committee on Internal Security, House of Representatives, 93rd Congress, 2nd Sess. Washington, D.C.: Government Printing Office, 1974.

Kelly, James; Brew, Douglas; and Zagorin, Adam. "Searching for Hit Teams." Time, 21 December 1981, pp. 16-20, 22.

King, Jere Clemens. The First World War. New York: Walker and Co., 1972.

Knox, Neal. "Testimony." In Omnibus Antiterrorism Act of 1979. Hearings Before the Committee on Governmental Affairs, Senate, 96th Congress, 1st Sess. Washington, D.C.: Government Printing Office, 1979.

Kupperman, Robert, and Trent, Darrell, eds. Terrorism: Threat, Reality, Response. Stanford, Calif.: Hoover Institution Press of Stanford University, 1979.

Laqueur, Walter. Terrorism: A Study of National and International Political Violence. Boston: Little, Brown and Co., 1977.

_____. "Turkey's Trials." New Republic, 11 October 1980, pp. 13-15.

_____, ed. The Terrorism Reader: A Historical Anthology. New York: New American Library, 1978.

Lasky, Melvin J. "Ulrike Meinhof and the Baader-Meinhof Gang." Encounter 44 (June 1975):7-23.

"Latest Worry: Terrorists Using High Technology." U.S. News & World Report, 14 March 1977, p. 69.

Lefebvre, Georges. The French Revolution. Vol. 2: From 1793 to 1799. Translated by John H. Stewart and James Friguglietti. New York: Columbia University Press, 1964.

Levin, Bob, with Donosky, Lea. "Death Wish in Ulster." Newsweek, 4 May 1981, pp. 40-41.

_____. "The Legacy of Bobby Sands." Newsweek, 18 May 1981, pp. 50-53.

_____. "Ulster's Days of Rage." Newsweek, 11 May 1981, pp. 38-41.

"Libyan Assassins Now After Reagan?" U.S. News & World Report, 14 December 1981, p. 5.

Liston, Robert A. Terrorism. Nashville, Tenn.: Thomas Nelson, 1977.

Livingstone, Neil C. "Terrorism: The International Connection." Army, December 1980, pp. 14-21.

Lowe, E. Nobles, and Shargel, Harry D., eds. Legal and Other Aspects of Terrorism. New York: Practicing Law Institute, 1979.

Luks, Allan. "Testimony." In Terrorism, Part 2. Hearings Before the Committee on Internal Security, House of Representatives, 93rd Congress, 2nd Sess. Washington, D.C.: Government Printing Office, 1974.

Martin, David C. Wilderness of Mirrors. New York: Harper and Row, 1980.

Martin, Everett G. "Latin America's Terrorist Network." Wall Street Journal, 15 April 1980, p. 25.

McGrath, Peter. "Reagan's Peace Offensive." Newsweek, 30 November 1981, pp. 30-33.

Mickolus, Edward F. "Negotiating for Hostages: A Policy Dilemma." In Contemporary Terrorism: Selected Readings, pp. 219-25. Edited by John D. Elliott and Leslie K. Gibson. Gaithersburg, Md.: International Association of Chiefs of Police, 1978.

Middleton, Drew. "Going the Military Route." New York Times Magazine, Special Edition, 1981, pp. 103-12.

Milbank, David L. International and Transnational Terrorism: Diagnosis and Prognosis. Washington, D.C.: Central Intelligence Agency, April 1976.

"The Month in Review." Current History 80 (October 1981): 349.

Morganthau, Tom, and Shannon, Elaine. "The Terrorist Hunt." Newsweek, 4 May 1981, p. 25.

Moss, Robert. "Terror: A Soviet Export." New York Times Magazine, 2 November 1980, pp. 42-47.

National Advisory Committee on Criminal Justice Standards and Goals. Disorders and Terrorism: Report of the Task Force on Disorders and Terrorism. Washington, D.C.: National Advisory Committee on Criminal Justice Standards and Goals, 1976.

National Republican Senatorial Committee. "Terrorism Threatens U.S. National Security." Special Report, Washington, D.C., May 1981, pp. 1-4.

Navasky, Victor. "Security and Terrorism." Nation 232 (14 February 1981):167-86.

Nazzaro, Pellegrino. "Order or Chaos in Italy?" Current History 77 (November 1979):172-74.

Neff, James. "Internal Security: Right Sees Threat, Left Charges McCarthyism." San Francisco Examiner & Chronicle, 13 September 1981, p. A-16.

New York Times. "America in Captivity: Points of Decision in the Hostage Crisis: An Inquiry by the New York Times." New York Times Magazine, Special Edition, 1981, pp. 1-40.

_____, ed. The Watergate Hearings: Break-In and Cover-Up. New York: Viking Press, 1973.

O'Ballance, Edgar. Language of Violence: The Blood Politics of Terrorism. San Rafael, Calif.: Presidio Press, 1979.

Oberdorfer, Don, and Schram, Martin. "Haig Believes a Reagan Aide Is Campaigning Against Him." Washington Post, 4 November 1981, pp. A-1, A-9.

Omang, Joanne. "Stirrings of Life Return to Love Canal." Washington Post, 9 November 1981, pp. A-1, A-2.

Parry, Albert. Terrorism: From Robespierre to Arafat. New York: Vanguard Press, 1976.

Perlmutter, Amos. "Targeting the Real Soviet-Backed Terrorist." Long Island Newsday, 16 April 1981, part II, p. 9-F.

Ponte, Lowell. "Terrorism's Monstrous New Age." Next 1 (July/August 1980):48-55.

"A President Under Wraps." U.S. News & World Report, 21 December 1981, p. 11.

President's Commission on the Assassination of President Kennedy. Report. Washington, D.C.: Government Printing Office, 1964.

Price, Raymond. With Nixon. New York: Viking Press, 1977.

Quainton, Anthony C. E. "Statement." In Hearings. Subcommittee on Aviation of the Committee on Public Works and Transportation, House of Representatives, 96th Congress, 1st Sess. Washington, D.C.: Government Printing Office, 28 February 1979.

_____. "Terrorism: Do Something! But What?" Department of State Bulletin 79 (September 1979):60-64.

_____. "Testimony." In Federal Capabilities in Crisis Management and Terrorism. Hearings Before the Subcommittee on Civil and Constitutional Rights, House of Representatives, 95th Congress, 2nd Sess. Washington, D.C.: Government Printing Office, 1978.

_____. "Testimony." In Omnibus Antiterrorism Act of 1979. Hearings Before the Committee on Governmental Affairs, Senate, 96th Congress, 1st Sess. Washington, D.C.: Government Printing Office, 1979.

_____. "U.S. Antiterrorism Program." Department of State Bulletin 80 (July 1980):75-77.

Rabe, Robert L. "Testimony." In Terrorism, Part 2. Hearings Before the Committee on Internal Security, House of Representatives, 93rd Congress, 2nd Sess. Washington, D.C.: Government Printing Office, 1974.

Reed, David. "Northern Ireland--the Endless War." Reader's Digest, July 1975, pp. 84-93.

Rogal, Kim, and Sciolino, Elaine. "The Kidnapped U.S. General." Newsweek, 28 December 1981, p. 46.

Rogers, William D. "Who's in Charge of Foreign Policy?" New York Times Magazine, 9 September 1979, pp. 44-50.

Rose, Gregory F. "The Terrorists Are Coming." Politics Today, July/August 1978, p. 52.

Rosenthal, A. M. "America in Captivity: A Preface." New York Times Magazine, Special Edition, 1981, pp. 33-35.

Sawyer, Kathy. "Police Push to Flush Out the Underground." Washington Post, 25 October 1981, p. A-2.

Seiberling, John E. "Question." In Federal Capabilities in Crisis Management and Terrorism. Hearings Before the Subcommittee on Civil and Constitutional Rights, House of Representatives, 95th Congress, 2nd Sess. Washington, D.C.: Government Printing Office, 1978.

Selzer, Michael. Terrorist Chic: an Exploration of Violence in the Seventies. New York: Hawthorn Books, 1979.

Shaw, P. D. "Extortion Threats--Analytic Techniques and Resources." Assets Protection 1 (Summer 1975):5-16.

Shulman, Marshall D. "Man Bites Dogma." Columbia, October 1981, pp. 17-20.

Smith, Hedrick. "An Assertive America." New York Times, 25 January 1981, p. 17.

_____. "Feuding Over Foreign Policy Roles Is Renewed Within Administration." New York Times, 24 March 1981, pp. 1, 6.

Smith, Terence. "Putting the Hostages' Lives First." New York Times Magazine, Special Edition, 1981, pp. 77-101.

Staar, Richard F. "Worldwide Terrorism: The Soviet Union
     Is at the Bottom of It." Los Angeles Times, 1 May
     1981, part II, p. 11.

Sterling, Claire. "The Terrorist Network." Atlantic
     Monthly, November 1978, pp. 37-51.

_____. The Terror Network: The Secret War of Inter-
     national Terrorism. New York: Holt, Rinehart and
     Winston and Reader's Digest Press, 1981.

Stevens, Georgiana G. The United States and the Middle
     East. New York: American Assembly, Columbia
     University, 1964.

Stohl, Michael, ed. The Politics of Terrorism. New
     York: Marcel Dekker, 1979.

Subject Guide to Books in Print, 1980-1981. New York:
     R. R. Bowker, 1980.

"Terrified of Television." Economist (London), 22 March
     1980, p. 59.

Thornton, Mary. "Attorney General Emphasizes Punishment and
     Deterrence." Washington Post, 29 October 1981,
     p. A-10.

_____. "GAO Criticizes Strike Force on Organized Crime."
     Washington Post, 7 December 1981, pp. A-1, A-5.

Trick, Marcia McKnight. "Chronology of Terroristic, Quasi-
     Terroristic, and Political Violence in the United
     States, January 1965 to March 1976." In Disorders
     and Terrorism: Report of the Task Force on Disorders
     and Terrorism, pp. 507-95. Washington, D.C.: National
     Advisory Committee on Criminal Justice Standards and
     Goals, 1976.

Turner, Stansfield. "The CIA Shouldn't Spy on Americans."
     Washington Post, 1 November 1981, p. C-7.

"Uncle Sam's Antiterrorism Plan." Security Management,
     February 1980, p. 41.

U.S. Congress. House. Committee on Internal Security.
     Terrorism, Parts 1, 2, 3, 4. Hearings Before the
     Committee on Internal Security, 93rd Congress, 2nd
     Sess., 1974.

_____. Subcommittee on Aviation. Hearings Before the Sub-
     committee on Aviation of the Committee on Public Works
     and Transportation, 96th Congress, 1st. Sess., 1979.

_____. Subcommittee on Civil and Constitutional Rights. Federal Capabilities in Crisis Management and Terrorism. Hearings Before the Subcommittee on Civil and Constitutional Rights, 95th Congress, 2nd Sess., 1978.

U.S. Congress. Senate. Committee on Governmental Affairs. An Act to Combat International Terrorism. Hearings Before the Committee on Governmental Affairs, 95th Congress, 2nd Sess., 1978.

_____. Committee on Governmental Affairs. Omnibus Antiterrorism Act of 1979. Hearings Before the Committee on Governmental Affairs, 96th Congress, 1st Sess., 1979.

U.S. Department of Justice. Hostage Situations. Quantico, Va.: Federal Bureau of Investigation Academy, January 1975.

U.S. Department of State. The Biographic Register, 1968-1969. Washington, D.C.: Department of State, 1969.

_____. "Department Statement," July 28, 1978. Department of State Bulletin 78 (September 1978):5.

_____. Significant Terrorist Incidents, 1970-1980. Washington, D.C.: Department of State, n.d.

_____. "U.S. Policy on Terrorism: Air Force Policy Letter for Commanders." Department of State Bulletin 79 (May 1979):31.

"U.S. Terrorism Policy Defined." Defense and Foreign Affairs Daily, Main Edition, part II, 8 April 1981, pp. 1-2.

Vance, Cyrus R. "Terrorism: Scope of the Threat and Need for Effective Legislation." Department of State Bulletin 78 (March 1978):54.

Velde, Richard W. "Testimony." In Terrorism, Part 4. Hearings Before the Committee on Internal Security, House of Representatives, 93rd Congress, 2nd Sess. Washington, D.C.: Government Printing Office, 1974.

Vinocur, John. "German Terrorists Pursue Fresh Targets with Old Strategies." New York Times, 20 September 1981, p. E-3.

Wattenberg, Ben J. "It's Time to Stop America's Retreat." New York Times Magazine, 22 July 1979, pp. 14-16, 68-69.

_____. _The Statistical History of the United States from Colonial Times to the Present_. New York: Basic Books, 1976.

Weisman, Steven R. "For America, A Painful Reawakening." _New York Times Magazine_, Special Edition, 1981, pp. 114-37.

Weissman, Steve. "Crying Wolf at Watergate." In _Big Brother and the Holding Company: The World Behind Watergate_, pp. 27-44. Palo Alto, Calif.: Ramparts Press, 1974.

White, Theodore H. _The Making of the President, 1968_. New York: Atheneum Publishers, 1969.

"Why Reagan Moved Against Libya's Qadhafi." _U.S. News & World Report_, 21 December 1981, p. 10.

Wilkinson, Paul. _Political Terrorism_. New York: John Wiley and Sons, 1974.

_____. "Still Working for the Extinction of Mankind." _Across the Board_, January 1981, pp. 27-30.

Wilson, C. _The Tupamaros: The Unmentionables_. Boston: Branden Press, 1974.

Wolff, Lester L. "Comments." In _International Terrorism: Legislative Initiatives_. Hearings Before the Committee on International Relations, House of Representatives, 95th Congress, 2nd Sess. Washington, D.C.: Government Printing Office, 1978.